BIRDWATCH

A Young Person's Introduction to Birding

by Mary MacPherson
illustrations by Virginia Douglas

Summerhill Press
Toronto

© 1988 Mary MacPherson
illustrations © 1988 Virginia Douglas
Second edition, revised

Published by Summerhill Press
Toronto, Ontario M4T 1A2

Distributed in Canada by
University of Toronto Press
5201 Dufferin Street
Downsview, Ontario M3H 5T8

Distributed in the United States by
Sterling Publishing
2 Park Avenue
New York, New York 10016

Cover photography by Albert Kuhnigk
Cover design by Rob McPhail
Text design by Michelle Maynes

Printed and bound in Canada

Canadian Cataloguing in Publication Data

MacPherson, Mary
     Birdwatch

Includes index.
ISBN 0-920197-57-4

1. Bird watching - Juvenile literature.
2. Birds - Juvenile literature. I. Douglas, Ginny,
1957-   . II Title.

QL677.5.M3 1988   j598'.07'234   C88-094721-7

For my parents

CONTENTS

BIRDWATCH

Stop what you are doing right now and look out the window. In no time at all you will see a bird. Whether you live in the city or the country, near mountains, rivers, lakes, or the coast, you can always observe birds in their natural habitat. For birds are found in every part of the world except where ice permanently covers the surface of the earth.

Bird watching, or birding, is the sport of observing wild birds in their own environment. It is an activity which offers the excitement of pursuing a wild creature, in order to observe it up close, combined with the fun of collecting, because we make lists of what we see.

Birds are our most visible form of wildlife. They are beautiful and fascinating. The more you observe birds the more they will arouse your curiosity and interest you in the environment. Their abundance gives the sport of birding variety unequalled by any other activity. Birding can be enjoyed throughout the year and throughout your lifetime, no matter where you are, no matter where you go, at any time of day, at night, in any kind of weather. You will also meet other bird watchers who will share their enthusiasm and knowledge with you.

Whether you are a beginner or a more experienced birder, whether the sport of birding is your main interest or you combine it with other activities like camping or hiking, whether you remain in your own backyard to observe birds, or travel the world, discovery and adventure are limited only by your imagination.

Chapter 1

BIRD WATCHING

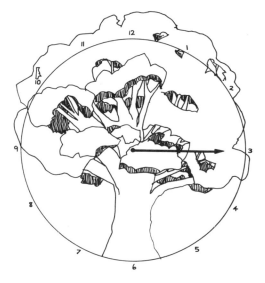

GETTING STARTED

Identifying birds is a matter of becoming familiar with them. Your best tools are your eyes and your ears. Watch and listen. For your own safety and enjoyment, bird watch with a friend. Two pairs of eyes and ears are often better than one.

The important thing while birding is to observe quietly. When you are outside, signal to fellow bird watchers by whistling. Speak in a soft voice. Use the clock technique to describe a bird's location to others; for example, you might say a bird is at "three o'clock" to indicate a bird directly ahead and to the right of you.

Move slowly and quietly. Make use of natural cover like bushes and tall grasses to hide in, and dress in nature's colors to blend with the surroundings. Wear earth tones, avoiding black, white, or fluorescent-colored clothing. Choose comfortable clothing. Wear a hat in summer for shade and in cooler seasons for warmth. Flat or low-heeled footwear is important for comfort as well as for safety. Big pockets and belt pouches come in handy for carrying equipment.

EQUIPMENT

NOTEBOOK AND PENCIL

Your notebook is possibly your most important tool in helping you to learn about birds. Make notes as you go. Don't expect to remember all the details when you get home—it's easy to forget. The information you record in the field will help you to accurately identify both familiar and new species.

Choose a pocket-size book that is easy to carry. It should have blank pages for making sketches and a durable cover (you may want to cover it in plastic) which will stand up to weather and wear-and-tear. Always work in pencil and never pen; a pencil will work in all weather conditions.

FIELD GUIDE

A field guide is essential for the beginner. It tells you when and where you can find which birds. Generally, a field guide gives a brief physical description of each bird, identifies similar species, describes the bird's voice, names its range (the geographical location in which it lives; for example, central Canada and northern United States), and its habitat (the vegetational area within the range; for example, prairies, dunes, and fields). A colored photograph or drawing is provided for easy identification, and range maps show the seasonal distribution of each species. Many field guides are devoted to a particular province, state, or region. If you don't already have a field guide, buy one that is written specifically for your area. Try to obtain the most recent publication available since the ranges of many species change markedly over time. The following field guides are recommended:

The Audubon Society Field Guide to North American Birds. Vol. I, by John Bull and John Farrand *The Audubon Society Field Guide to North American Birds. Vol. II*, by Miklos D.F. Udvardy

Birds of North America, by Chandler S. Robbins, Bertel Bruun, and Herbert S. Zim

A Field Guide to the Birds East of the Rockies, by Roger Tory
  Peterson

Field Guide to the Birds of North America, Shirley L. Scott, ed.

A Field Guide to the Western Birds, by Roger Tory Peterson

Simon & Schuster Guide to the Birds of the World, by
  Gianfranco Bologna, John Bull, ed.

BINOCULARS

Binoculars increase the enjoyment of birding and are
essential equipment, especially for activities like hawk
watching. If you can't borrow a pair, save your allowance
and buy some. It is a worthwhile investment. There is a
great variety to choose from. Try out a number of models
and keep the following guidelines in mind.

The two most important features are the power of magnification and the sharpness of the image. These are ex-
pressed by two numbers usually located near the eyepiece.
The most popular binoculars among birders are 7 X 35.

The first number (in this case 7) is the power or magnification. Binoculars work by magnifying the image of the
object, making it appear closer than it is. Binoculars with a

power of 7 make a bird appear seven times closer to you. The larger the number, the greater the magnification.

The second number (in this case 35) is the diameter of the largest lens measured in millimeters. This number determines the amount of light let in, affecting how well you see the image. The larger the number, the clearer the image will be.

Don't assume that bigger is better. With greater magnification and clarity, the binoculars become heavier and more sensitive to movement, even the slightest quiver of your hands. Choose a pair you are able to hold steady for several minutes.

When using binoculars, adjust the eyepieces so they are the same distance apart as your eyes. You should see only one image. At first you may have difficulty using binoculars, especially when trying to look at moving birds. Begin by focusing on objects that will not move away and adjust the focus until it suits you. Remember that the "field of vision" of the binoculars is much narrower than that of your eye so when you see a bird, keep watching it while you raise the binoculars to your eyes. This way you will be able to focus your binoculars on the right place.

OPTIONAL EQUIPMENT

Checklist

A checklist tells you which birds can be found in a particular geographical area, whether a bird is commonly or rarely seen, and in what season. Made of stiff paper, a checklist fits easily into your field guide or notebook. It is usually available for your area, or places you are visiting, from the local birding or naturalist club.

Camera

Collecting birds, as once practised, is now prohibited by law. Current records of bird sightings are based upon bird watchers' observations and photographs. You may wish to collect your own photographs of birds, their nests, and their eggs, or you may take pictures just to have a visual memory of the day's outing.

For birding, use a 35 mm camera. If you are buying a camera, stay with the brand names (Minolta, Pentax, and Nikon). Two types of lenses will accommodate most of your pictures. A macro lens with a focal length between 50 and 55 mm will allow you to take close-up pictures within one foot. A telephoto lens, between 150 and 200 mm, is for long-range shooting.

The best time of year to photograph birds is at the height of the nesting season. In the southern United States it is May; farther north and in Canada it is June. Some birds, however, like chickadees and owls, begin nesting as early as February or March.

Tape Recorder

A lightweight, pocket-size tape recorder is useful for recording spoken field notes, recording bird sounds, and playing pre-recorded bird sounds. Verbal field notes can be recorded and then transcribed into your notebook later at home.

Recording bird sounds can help you to identify different species. Two birds that look alike may sound different. You may wish to build a tape library of bird sounds since about half the songs of the world's species are still unrecorded!

Playing your own or commercially pre-recorded bird sounds in the field will often attract that particular species. For a list of suggested records and tapes, see the section on "Recorded Bird Sounds" in the bibliography.

Remember, birds are most vocal during spring breeding season when males are calling to attract females and to defend their territory.

WHERE TO GO

WHEN

During daylight hours, you can bird watch almost any-
where. In the warmer months, birds are most active just
after sunrise and before sunset, and less so at midday. In
winter, when food is less plentiful, birds are busy throughout the day. Birds are most vocal during migration, calling
to keep their flock together, and during courtship in spring.
These are also the times when birds are easiest to spot.
During migration, more birds are airborne, and in mating
season, their feathers are more colorful.

Waterfowl are generally active all day, and shorebirds
of the sea are most visible at low tide when the shore animals that they feed upon are exposed in the sand. Soaring
birds, which glide on rising columns of warm air, are rarely
seen early in the day.

WHERE

The ideal place for birding is where two or more biotic
communities, areas of different types of vegetation, come
together. These areas are called ecotones.

There are many ecological combinations which provide

the conditions of an ecotone. Look for birds where woodland meets a marsh or a field, at a lake or seashore edged by a forest, or where a field is next to an area of low shrubs.

On these open "edges," sunlight stimulates a variety of plant life. Birds—as well as other animals—eat in this area while remaining close to the safety of cover.

Going on an outing to the country will enable you to observe birds in a variety of ecotones. Bird observatories, bird sanctuaries, conservation areas, zoos, and national, state, and provincial parks are ideal for birding because they are places specifically chosen for their particular type or number of biotic communities.

Ecotones exist within cities too. Explore your own backyard or your neighbor's where grass meets ground cover, hedges, and trees. Local parks are places where lakes, ponds, streams, and marshes come together with grasses, bushes, and trees. If you live near a lake, a river, an ocean port, or a mountain range, there will be an even greater number of ecotones to attract birds.

BIRD IDENTIFICATION

Bird identification is a process of elimination. There are three basic steps. First, check details of the location you will be bird watching in; second, note the bird's shape and behavior; finally, and only if necessary, consider the bird's field marks. This logical, systematic process takes you from the general to the specific.

LOCATION

Before going outside, spend some time "personalizing" your field guide. Go through it page by page and identify with a marker or highlighter the birds that inhabit your geographical area. This exercise will familiarize you with the birds you can expect to see and will eliminate all the species that do not live where you will be bird watching. Remember too that many birds migrate and therefore have seasonal ranges. They live in different areas at different times of the year. Consult the range maps in your field guide and your local checklist.

HABITAT

Determining a bird's habitat—that is, the specific area of vegetation in which it lives—helps you to eliminate more species within a geographical location. If your outing is to a marsh, the birds you see will be different from those that inhabit a woodland or a field. Also, the level of vegetation will be a significant clue to the bird's identity. Birds generally build nests near where they search for food. The four levels that birds occupy are: ground level, undergrowth and low bush level, high bush and low tree branch level, high tree branch and tree top level. See the next two pages for some examples of birds occupying these levels.

So, before you even see a bird, you know where it lives. Now you are ready to go birding. In the field, you will begin by noting the shape and behavior of each species you see.

Shape

The shape or form of a bird is a more reliable clue to its identity than its color or field marks, which can be distorted by vegetation, poor light, and seasonal changes in plumage. The shape of a duck, owl, crow, and hawk are illustrated here. Already you can identify four families of birds. Consult your field guide to learn the basic shapes of each bird family in your geographical area. The three features of a bird which distinguish its shape are its wings, bill, and feet. These are also clues to where it lives and what it eats.

DUCK

OWL

CROW

HAWK

BIRD HABITAT LEVELS

Ground level 2"–1' (51– 305 mm)	*Undergrowth and* *low bush level* 2'–5' (.6–1.5 m)	*High bush and* *low branch level* 5'–15' (1.5–4.5 m)
black and white warbler		
Canada warbler	brown thrasher	blue-headed vireo
hermit thrush	cardinal	blue jay
junco	catbird	cedar waxwing
Nashville warbler	chestnut-sided warbler	chipping sparrow
ovenbird	field sparrow	cuckoo
pine-woods sparrow	hooded warbler	golden-crowned kinglet
towhee	indigo bunting	goldfinch
veery	mockingbird	grosbeak
white-throated sparrow	mourning warbler	kingbird
whip-poor-will	white-eyed vireo	magnolia warbler
woodcock	winter wren	mourning dove
	yellow-breasted chat	myrtle warbler
		red-eyed vireo
		redstart
		robin
		scarlet tanager

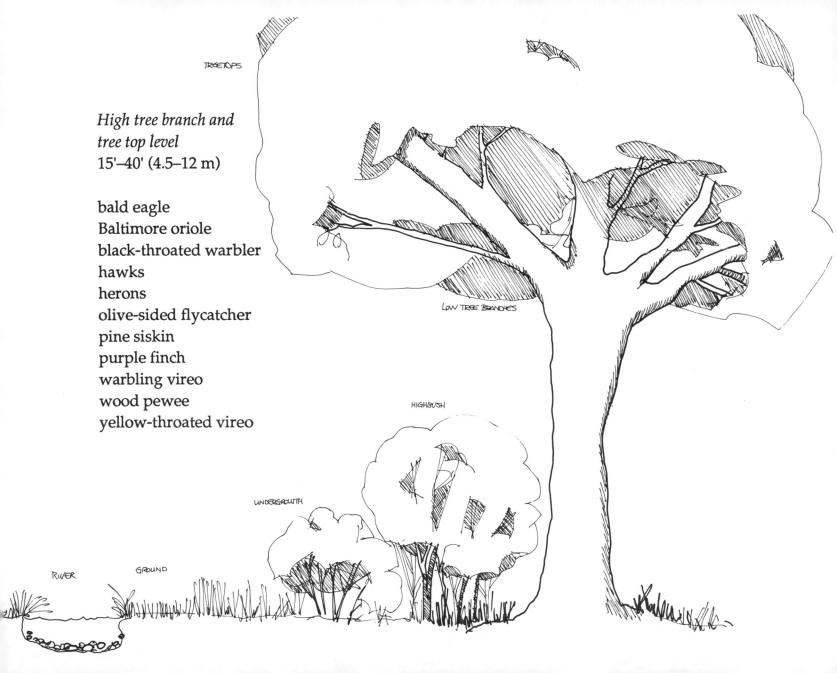

TREETOPS

*High tree branch and
tree top level
15'–40' (4.5–12 m)*

bald eagle
Baltimore oriole
black-throated warbler
hawks
herons
olive-sided flycatcher
pine siskin
purple finch
warbling vireo
wood pewee
yellow-throated vireo

LOW TREE BRANCHES

HIGHBUSH

UNDERGROWTH

RIVER   GROUND

BUTEO

ACCIPITER

FALCON

WINGS

If you can tell from its overall shape that a bird is a hawk, its wing shape will help you decide if it's a buteo (long, broad wings), a falcon (long, pointed wings), or an accipiter (short, rounded wings).

BILL

A bird's bill can be long or short, curved or hooked, crossed, upturned, downturned, spearlike or spoonlike. Each is adapted to eating a specific food. A good look at the shape of a bird's bill will tell you if it's a finch (a short, thick bill), a swallow (a flat bill with a broad base), a warbler (a long, thin bill), or a blackbird (a long, pointed bill). Here are some of the bill types you might encounter.

FINCH

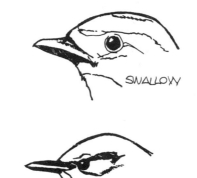

SWALLOW

WARBLER

BLACKBIRD

generalist: long and pointed bill for catching insects and worms, heavy enough for cracking seeds

seed eater: short, thick bill for cracking seeds

seed extractor: crossed bill for taking seeds from cones

insect eater: long, thin bill for picking insects from leaves or bark

insect catcher: flat bill with a broad base that opens very wide for catching insects

meat eater: hooked bill for tearing prey

fish and frog catcher: long, pointed bill for spearing prey

FEET

The legs and feet of birds are specialized as well. Their form indicates their function. Perching birds, like robins, have four toes that extend from the same level on the leg. Three toes point forward and one back. This arrangement enables them to walk, hop, and perch.

Unlike perching birds, most woodpeckers have two toes forward, one back, and one to the side. This enables them to climb with great skill.

The feet of predators, such as owls, hawks, and eagles, have sharp talons for killing and carrying off their prey. Ducks have webbed feet for swimming, and grebes have lobed feet for diving. Shorebirds, such as sandpipers, have small hind toes, well adapted for walking.

AMERICAN ROBIN
FOR WALKING AND
PERCHING

WOODPECKER
FOR CLIMBING

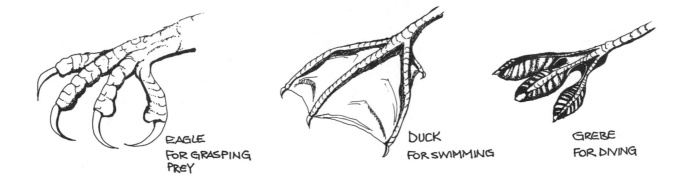

EAGLE
FOR GRASPING
PREY

DUCK
FOR SWIMMING

GREBE
FOR DIVING

BEHAVIOR

Related groups of birds tend to have the same "air" or "manner." Behavior often identifies a bird's family or genus, but more frequently indicates its species. Whether a bird is on the ground or in flight, its behavior provides clues to its identity.

Consider, for example, the flight characteristics of birds: swallows sweep over the ground and water, making quick turns and circles in the air; kites and buzzards drift in circles, their wings outstretched and motionless; owls move as if buoyant, lighter than the air; red-winged blackbirds in a flock fly with a short series of flaps, pause a few seconds as if stalled, and flap again; a flock of starlings flaps continuously. Some birds, like sparrows, fly in straight lines; others, like goldfinches, fly up and down. Many birds travel in groups, others in pairs, some alone.

SIZE

Identifying birds by their size is easier when you can compare the size of the unknown bird with the size of a bird you know. This method should only be used when you can see both birds at the same time and they are relatively close together. When a bird is isolated or at a distance, it is difficult to accurately judge its size. (In California, signs warn people watching for condors that the birds are often over-looked because they are mistaken for airplanes.)

FIELD MARKS

Now that you have narrowed down the number of species within one family that your bird might belong to, you can now consider its field marks. Field marks are the physical points that distinguish one species from another species it closely resembles. Are there wing bars or tail bars, an eye ring or a breast spot? Now is the time to consult your field guide for positive identification, or with good field notes you can wait until you get home.

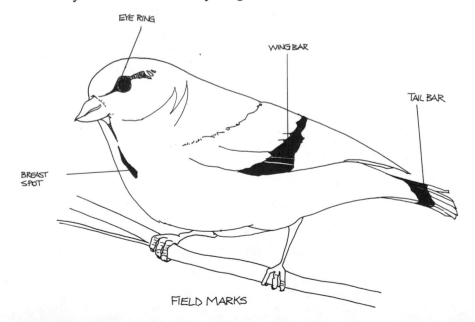

FIELD MARKS

FIELD NOTES

Use your notebook to record the following information: date; time of day; location; habitat; weather conditions; list of familiar birds (with notes on behavior, flock size, sex (♀ is the symbol for female, ♂ is the symbol for male); bird calls; and a sketch of unidentified birds (along with a physical description and notes on behavior).

When it comes to "mystery" birds, record as much information as you can and be as accurate as possible. So you will not miss anything, begin with a description of the bird's head and work your way back to the tail. Later, at home, you can take the time to research in detail what you have observed. Don't be discouraged if a bird moves away too quickly or is too well camouflaged. Chances are that you will see the bird again that day or perhaps on another outing. With practice, you will improve your skills of observation.

Develop your notebook to suit your own needs. For example, in the back of your book, you might want to create a list of species local to your area, as well as your own personal "life list," adding the different species you have identified on each outing.

FIELD SKETCH

To draw a field sketch of a bird, begin with an oval shape. All birds, regardless of size, from owls to chickadees, have oval-shaped bodies. What makes them appear different are their wings, tail, legs, and head.

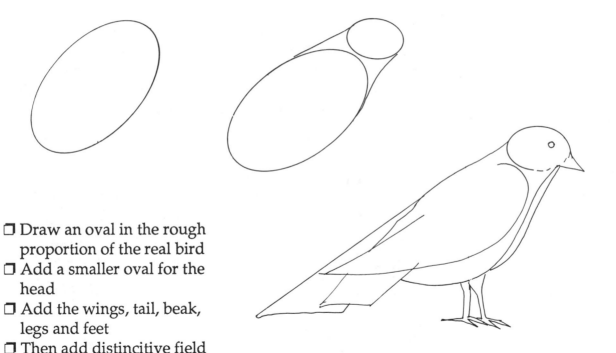

- ❑ Draw an oval in the rough proportion of the real bird
- ❑ Add a smaller oval for the head
- ❑ Add the wings, tail, beak, legs and feet
- ❑ Then add distincitive field marks

VOICE IDENTIFICATION

Each species of bird has a distinctive call or voice. For the seasoned listener, this can be the best means of bird identification. However, recognizing the call is a skill that comes only with time and experience.

To learn bird sounds, begin by listening to birds you can see and already know. Then move on to unfamiliar birds you can see. Being able to both see and hear the bird makes it easier to remember the calls.

Birding with someone skilled in voice identification is one of the best ways of learning unfamiliar calls, especially those of birds you hear but cannot see. This is just one of the many advantages of joining a bird club. Or you can make recordings or take field notes, which, with more experience, you will be able to identify.

There are several ways of taking field notes. Occasionally, a bird will call in a way that can be matched to human words, and the call can be written the way it sounds. For example, the white-throated sparrow sings *poor-sam-pea-body-peabody-peabody;* the robin calls *cheerily-cheerily;* and the wood peewee says *pee-a-wee;* the chickadee sings *phe-be-be;* and the junco says *sweet-sweet-sweet.*

Other sounds are best represented by written symbols. You can invent your own shorthand. A thin line can repre-

sent a fine hissing note like that of the golden-crowned
kinglet or the cedar waxwing. A broader line can be used
for a fuller whistle like that of the chickadee, and small
circles for a mellower-sounding junco. A straight line can
represent a clear note, a spiral line a warble, and a wavy
line a trembling note. For a continuous song, connect the
lines. If there are pauses in the song, leave spaces in your
drawing.

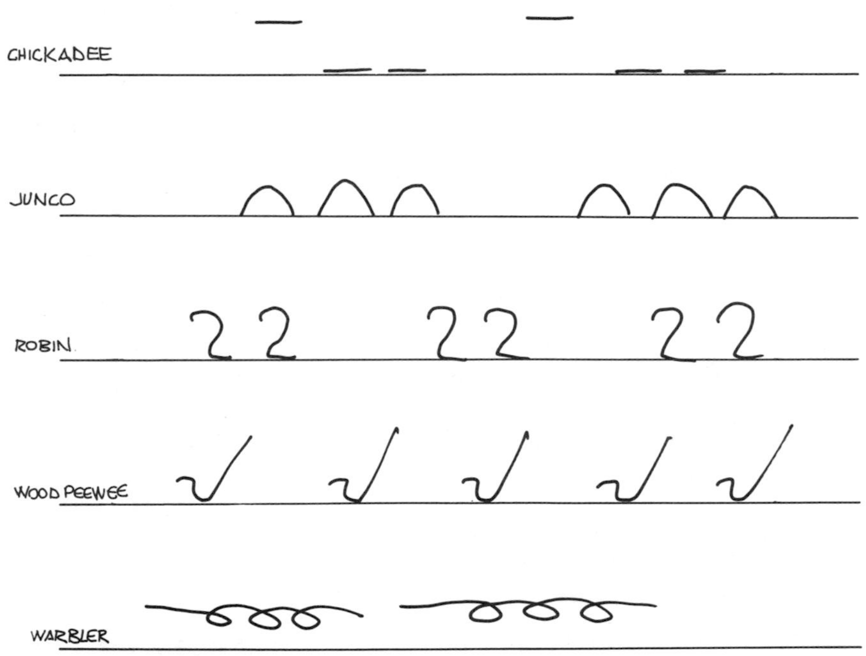

CHICKADEE

JUNCO

ROBIN

WOOD PEEWEE

WARBLER

Another way to familiarize yourself with birds sounds is to listen to nature records and tapes available in record shops, nature specialty stores, and public libraries. Comparing your own recordings or your field notes to the commercial recordings may help you identify your mystery birds. The following records and tapes are recommended:

Field Guide to Bird Songs, 2nd ed., by Roger Tory Peterson

A Field Guide to the Bird Songs of Eastern and Central North America, Cornell Laboratory of Ornithology, Cornell University

A Field Guide to Western Bird Songs, Cornell Laboratory of Ornithology, Cornell University*Field Guide to Bird Songs.* 2nd ed., by Roger Tory Peterson

Nature Sounds of the Northwest, by K.J. Hall and Peter R.B. Ward. Vol. 1, *Birds of the Dry Interior;* Vol. 2, *Birds of the Estuaries and Mountains*

Sound of Nature Series, by Dr. W.W.H. Gunn. *Songs of Spring; Warblers; Finches; Prairie Spring; Thrushes, Wrens and Mockingbirds*

Voices of the Loon, by William Barklow

Warblers of North America, Cornell Laboratory of Ornithology, Cornell University

Chapter 2

ATTRACTING BIRDS

Eight hundred and thirty-five species of birds spend at least part of the year in North America. Attracting birds to your home is one of the best ways to observe and learn about them. Birds require food and water, shelter from predators, and a place to raise their young. There are many ways you can attract them and provide for them in every season.

IN FALL

The fall, when birds begin to gather and migrate, is the time to clean out used nest boxes that birds have left to rid the boxes of parasites and prepare them for the following

spring. It is also the best time to plan your winter feeding station. That way you will be ready for your guests when the cold weather arrives.

First, select a sheltered area that will be easy to reach if there is snow on the ground. Bushes, hedges, shrubs, and trees provide birds with protection from predators and shelter the feeders from weather. Select an area you can view from a window.

Next, plan your feeding-station so that you can collect materials and assemble the feeders ahead of time. To attract the maximum number of birds, a feeding station should consist of: a hanging seed dispenser, a ground feeder, a suet container, and water. These will provide the birds with good nutrition.

SEED DISPENSERS

All garden-variety birds (except hummingbirds) will eat seeds, even those who prefer insects. Seeds are high in protein, fats, and carbohydrates. If possible, have at least two types of dispensers, one for sunflower seeds and one for wild birdseed mix. If you are limited to one seed dispenser, fill it with sunflower seeds only. This is the number-one choice of most songbirds.

There are three types of sunflower seeds: the largest is

gray-striped; the medium size is black-striped; the smallest is black. The "black oil" sunflower, as it is called, is the favorite because it has more oil and a thinner shell which is easier for birds to crack. Sunflower hearts (seeds with the shells removed) are popular too, but much more expensive.

Commercial seed dispensers are well made and should last many years, but several types of dispensers can be made each year from items found in your home. A plastic bleach container (make sure it's well washed), a cardboard milk carton, a wooden basket, or a coconut shell are just some of the items you can convert to hold seeds. Use your imagination and see what other household items you can use. Directions for making bird feeders can be found in the "Fall projects" section.

GROUND FEEDERS

Many birds naturally feed on or near the ground. These include the black-capped chickadee, blue jay, brown-headed cowbird, cardinal, common grackle, crow, dark-eyed junco, mourning dove, northern bobwhite, pigeon, red-winged blackbird, ring-necked pheasant, rufous-sided towhee, scrub jay, and sparrow (American tree, fox, house, song, white-crowned, white-throated).

A ground feeder will attract the greatest number and

variety of birds. You will also be able to observe more kinds of bird behavior that cannot take place at hanging feeders because of the limited space there.

You can create a ground feeder by scattering feed directly onto the ground. The larger the area, the more birds you will attract. You can also use a tray-type feeder, placed on the ground or slightly elevated. It can be made of wood or plastic, should be approximately three inches (8 cm) deep, and have holes drilled in it for drainage. Gravel or sand placed on the bottom will allow for drainage after rain and snow storms. Ground feeders should be placed near shrubs or bushes so birds can take cover if predators appear.

The best type of feed to use is cracked corn. It is inexpensive and appeals to ground-feeding birds. If you have a choice, choose the "finely" cracked corn.

Ground feeders sometimes attract squirrels as well. However, this diverts them from eating the more expensive feed in your seed dispensers.

The most economical way to buy bird seed is in large quantities. Store seed in clean, dry containers, like trash cans. Clean your feeders regularly and throw out old or moldy food.

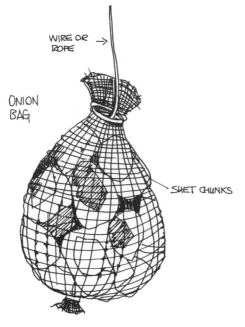

WIRE OR ROPE →

ONION BAG

SUET CHUNKS

SUET CONTAINERS

Suet, which is raw beef fat, may be obtained from your grocer. Suet provides birds with energy and warmth and is required only in the cold winter months. Suet is a favorite food of the chickadee (black-capped, Carolina), mocking-bird, nuthatch (red-breasted, white-breasted), starling, tufted titmouse, and woodpecker (downy, hairy, red-bel-lied, redheaded).

Mesh bags, such as onion bags, make great suet contain-ers, as do throw-away plastic or paper cups. (Never use wire mesh or metal screening, which can injure birds.) A log with holes drilled in it is also a good suet dispenser.

Suet feeders can be hung from the branches of a tree, another feeder, a porch railing or balcony, or can be at-tached to a tree trunk. Keep suet out of the reach of dogs, and be sure to secure it well so squirrels and large birds can't take the whole piece.

WATER

Birds require water in every season for drinking and bathing. Provide water by making a bird bath. Use a tray, a pie plate, the lid of a garbage can, or a similar container. Add flat stones for wading. A bird bath should contain no more than three inches (8 cm) of water. It may be on the ground or raised, and it should always be in the sun.

FALL PROJECTS

☐ Clean out used nest boxes.

☐ Select a sheltered area for your feeding station.

☐ Collect materials for making feeders: milk cartons, bleach bottles, muffin trays, six-quart (6-L) wooden baskets, or coconut shells for seeds, onion bags for suet. You will need strong twine to hang the feeders.

☐ Make bird feeders: With scissors, cut an opening in a milk carton or a bleach bottle as shown in the illustration. Muffin trays may simply be filled with seeds and used as a ground feeder. A six-quart (6-L) wooden basket, turned on its side and filled with seeds, provides a sheltered feeder. It is best to nail it to a fence top or other flat surface to keep it steady. Cut a coconut shell in half, suspend it from a tree, balcony or porch railing with strong twine, and fill with seeds. The birds will also enjoy eating the coconut.

☐ Gather pine cones for coating with suet, seed and peanut butter mixtures. Directions for making pine cone treats are in the "Winter projects" section.

☐ Gather food for winter feeding:

• Collect nuts such as acorns, beechnuts, chestnuts, and walnuts. Store in a dry place until winter.

• Collect fruit such as apples and crabapples from neglected trees and orchards. Store them in a cool place until

← WIRE OR ROPE

MILK

MILK CARTON

STRAWS MAKE GREAT PERCHES

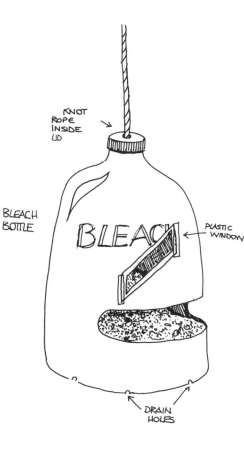

KNOT
ROPE
INSIDE
LID

BLEACH
BOTTLE

BLEACH

PLASTIC
WINDOW

DRAIN
HOLES

winter, and serve sliced, with the seeds exposed.

• Collect seeds from fruits and vegetables such as pumpkin, squash, and canteloupe. Wash and dry the seeds. Store with nuts in a dry place.

• Gather seeds from trees such as alder, ash, maple, and birch. Store in a dry place until winter.

• Clip the heads of wildflowers or flowers from your garden once the heads have wilted and turned brown. You might choose zinnias, chrysanthemums, marigolds and black-eyed Susans. Place the flower heads in a paper bag and store in a dry place. In winter, when they are fully dried, either shake the heads to separate the seeds or place the whole head in the feeder or on the ground.

IN WINTER

Birds are creatures of habit. Once you begin to feed them you should continue to do so throughout the winter if you want to maintain as many visitors as possible. If you are away for a week or two, your birds will not starve. They will just spend more time at other neighborhood feeders. It may take a little time to entice them back when you return.

Check your feeders twice a day, early in the morning and just before dusk. Birds are most active in the earliest part of the morning; they rest at midday, then feed again in the afternoon. With the type of food you serve, you can attract the birds of your choice while discouraging others!

FAVORITE FOODS

apples and crabapples	blue jays
buckwheat	cardinals, crows, mourning doves, ring-necked pheasants, ruffed grouse, sparrows
coconut	chickadees
corn (whole, cracked, meal)	doves (band-tailed, mourning, rock), Canada geese, cardinals, common grackles, cowbirds, crows, evening grosbeaks, flickers, ravens, ring-necked pheasants, rufous-sided towhees, slate-colored juncos, woodpeckers (hairy, red-bellied)
currants	bluebirds, brown thrashers, robins, ruffed grouse
millet	brown-headed cowbirds, Canada geese, cardinals, goldfinch, mallards, mourning doves, pigeons (rock dove), purple finches, redpolls, slate-colored juncos, sparrows
oats (crushed, rolled, porridge)	blackbirds, cardinals, grackles, grosbeaks, ring-necked pheasants, ruffed grouse, sparrows, starlings
peanuts	blackbirds, cardinals, catbirds, chickadees, crows, nuthatches, pigeons, purple finches, robins, slate-colored juncos, sparrows, starlings, tufted titmice, wrens, woodpeckers

raisins	bluebirds
rapeseed	goldfinches, mourning doves, purple finches, redpolls, slate-colored juncos
rice (cooked, uncooked, white, brown)	cardinals, ducks, geese, red-winged blackbirds, rock doves, slate-colored juncos, sparrows
safflower seeds	cardinals
seeds (fruit, vegetable)	blue jays, cardinals, chickadees, nuthatches
sorghum (cultivated)	bluejays, cardinals, grackles, mourning doves, slate-colored juncos
suet	all insect-eating birds
sunflower seeds	almost all birds, especially cardinals, chickadees (black-capped, boreal, chestnut-backed), grackles, mourning doves, nuthatches, pine siskins, purple finches, rose-breasted grosbeaks, slate-colored juncos, sparrows, tufted titmice
sunflower hearts	American goldfinches, common grackles

WINTER PROJECTS

☐ Collect leftovers each day from your own kitchen or your school cafeteria. Be sure none of the food is moldy. This can be harmful to birds. Leftovers might include crumbs, toast, breakfast cereals, crackers, dog biscuits and meal, donuts, mashed potatoes, muffins, pastry-crust crumbs, peanut butter, popcorn, fruit, and vegetables. Place them in ground feeders or on windowsills or sprinkle them on the snow. In place of suet, collect kitchen fat in a soup can.

☐ Make pine cone treats with suet, peanut butter, and seeds. Keep suet refrigerated or frozen before use. To prepare suet, bring it to room temperature. With the help of an adult, put it through a meat grinder or a food processor. Melt the fat over low heat until it is a smooth liquid. Then spoon the suet onto pine cones. Coat the pine cone with seeds, and allow to cool. Apply another layer of suet and seeds, and let cool. Build the cone with as many layers as you like.

Or, using a knife or a spoon, coat a pine cone with peanut butter and roll it in seeds. Tie a string to the stem of the pine cone and hang it outside.

☐ Make string food and decorate the trees outside the way you would a Christmas tree. Tie together peanuts in the shell, or string any number of foods such as cheese cubes, donuts, dried fruit, popcorn, and raisins.

❑ Take a bird survey:
- Compile a list of each type of bird attracted to your feeder.
- Vary the type of food you serve and make a list of the birds attracted by each food.
- With the help of a friend, take a count of the number of birds visiting your feeder in an hour, in a morning, in an afternoon, in a day.
- Compile other types of bird lists: birds seen in your backyard; birds seen from your backyard; birds seen from a bedroom window; birds seen on television; birds seen from a moving car; a travel list; a lifetime-world list.
- Organize a winter bird walk. With a group of friends, walk through your neighborhood to see how many different species of birds you can identify.
- Organize the members of your class or other group to make a bird calendar. On a large roll of paper, draw four vertical columns and title them "Name of bird," "Name of Observer," "Place Where Bird Was Seen," and "Date Bird Was First Seen." At the end of each term or the end of the school year, add up the total

number of birds reported by each person to see who identified the most birds.

☐ Draw bird tracks from prints you see in the snow, around your feeders, or on trees. Draw on cardboard instead of paper for easier handling outside. Take careful measurements so you can reproduce the tracks in life size.

First draw the general layout of the print. For example, are there three toes forward and one back (a perching bird), or two toes forward and two back (a climbing bird)? Measure the length of each toe print; the distance between each toe; the distance between running, walking, and hopping steps. Be sure to note also the condition of the snow in which the prints were made (light, fresh snow, wet snow, and so on).

Take your measurements and sketches inside and reproduce the tracks in life size. Observe the birds at your feeder and see if you can match the prints with the correct bird.

☐ Build a bird house. See "Nest boxes" in the next section.

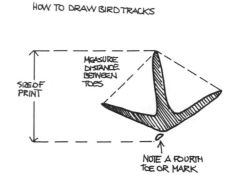

HOW TO DRAW BIRD TRACKS

SIZE OF PRINT

MEASURE DISTANCE BETWEEN TOES

NOTE A FOURTH TOE OR MARK

IN SPRING

Spring is an important time to feed birds because they require a great deal of energy during spring migration. Your feeding station will provide a good supplement to the insects, worms, and plant sprouts beginning to push up through the ground. Now is the time to stop suet feeding, because the milder temperatures turn suet rancid. Continue seed feeding until the end of April.

By April, nesting season usually begins or is well under way for some species. At this time, birds are no longer as dependent upon you for food as they were in winter. However, it is enjoyable to feed birds year-round. You can look forward to adult birds bringing their families to your feeders. You can also invite them into your garden by supplying nest boxes and nesting materials.

Nest boxes

In North America, several dozen species of birds nest in holes or cavities. Some of these birds include:

American kestrel	prothonotary warbler
barn owl	red-breasted nuthatch
barred owl	screech owl
bluebird	starling
brown creeper	tree sparrow
chickadee	tree swallow
crested flycatcher	tufted titmouse
English sparrow	white-breasted nuthatch
great horned owl	wood duck
house wren	woodpecker

Normally, the birds dig the cavities out of the soft wood fibres of decayed stumps and trees. However, fewer natural sites are available each year. Decaying trees are cut down for firewood or are removed because they are considered hazardous. Consequently, the population of cavity-nesting birds has declined in recent years. Providing nest boxes for cavity-nesting birds can reverse this trend.

A nest box should be in place as early in spring as possible, especially ones intended for early nesting birds like nuthatches and chickadees. Although nesting does not usually begin until April, a chickadee will begin preparing a nest cavity in February. Nest boxes put up after the beginning of April may not be occupied until the following year. If you plan to build your own nest box, start in the winter so it will be ready in plenty of time.

Some birds, like purple martins, nest in colonies in a multiple-unit birdhouse. However, single-compartment boxes are the easiest to build and the most frequently used by birds. The basic design for a single-compartment nest box is standard, but the size and location of the box will vary according to the species you wish to attract. See the chart on page 50 for the dimensions of nest boxes for some species of birds with the height at which they should be placed above ground.

BASIC NESTBOX

ROOF HINGED FOR EASY ACCESS TO NEST. NAILED DOWN ON FAR SIDE.

AIR VENTS

PROPER HOLE

AIR VENTS

Step-by-step plans for building birdhouses are available in books like:

30 Birds That Will Build in Bird Houses, by R.B Layton

102 Bird Houses, Feeders You Can Make, by Hi Sibley

Early nesters, like starlings and sparrows, will often take over boxes intended for other species. Cover the entrance of the house until the species you desire is sighted in your neighborhood.

To protect your nest box from predators, do not attach a perch or a platform on the outside near the entrance. If you place your box on a pole, attach an inverted, cone-shaped squirrel guard, or make a large circular barrier out of aluminum.

Sheet aluminum is available at most hardware and lumber stores. You need a piece between 14 and 20 inches (35 and 50 cm) wide. The length should be the same as the width, forming a square. With the help of an adult, cut off the corners to make a circle. Set the circle under the nest box. The aluminum may also be cut into strips and wrapped around the upper two feet (35 cm) of the pole. Keep the pole away from trees to stop cats, squirrels, and raccoons from jumping onto the roof of the nest box.

DIMENSIONS OF
NEST BOXES

SPECIES	FLOOR OF CAVITY inches (cm)	DEPTH OF CAVITY inches (cm)	HEIGHT OF ENTRANCE ABOVE FLOOR inches (cm)	DIAMETER OF ENTRANCE inches (cm)	HEIGHT ABOVE GROUND feet (m)
barn owl	10 x 18 (25 x 46)	15–18 (38–46)	4 (10)	6 (15)	12–18 (4–6)
bluebird	5x5 (13 x 13)	8 (20)	6 (15)	1 1/2 (4)	5–10 (1.5–3)
chickadee	4x4 (10x10)	8–10 (20–25)	6–8 (15–20)	1 1/8 (3)	6–15 (2–5)
downy woodpecker	4x4 (10x10)	9–12 (23–30)	6–8 (15–20)	1 1/4 (3.2)	6–20 (2–6)
house wren	4x4 (10x10)	6–8 (15–20)	1–6 (2.5–15)	1–1 1/4 (2.5–3)	6–10 (2–3)

Drill a few small holes in the sides, near the top, for ventilation, and in the floor, close to the walls, for drainage.

Be sure that the roof of the box can be easily removed to allow annual cleaning and occasional viewing and photography of the nest, eggs, and young. When the birds stop taking nesting materials into the box, the nest is complete and the eggs will soon be laid. Do not inspect the box during the first five days when the eggs are incubating. The adult birds are liable to abandon the nest if disturbed at this time.

RECORD-KEEPING

Keep records of spring arrivals, nesting, and departure dates for your own year-to-year comparison.

When you become adept at record-keeping, you may qualify to participate in the national Nest Record Card Program.

The keeping of nest records on a national scale originated in England. Information is gathered about the size of the nest, the materials it is made of, what is in the nest, the geographical location, habitat, and type of tree the nest is contained in. In North America, you may obtain cards by writing to Canada's provincial museums or to Cornell University:

British Columbia, Yukon
Bird and Mammal Division
B.C. Provincial Museum
Victoria, B.C.
V8W 1A1

Alberta, Saskatchewan, Manitoba
Manitoba Museum of Man
and Nature,
190 Rupert Ave.,
Winnipeg, Man.
R3B 0N2

Ontario
Department of Ornithology,
Royal Ontario Museum,
100 Queen's Park,
Toronto, Ont.
M5S 2C6

Quebec
Ornithology Section,
National Museum of
Natural Sciences,
Metcalfe and McLeod
Streets,
Ottawa, Ont.
K1A 0M8

New Brunswick, Nova Scotia,
Prince Edward Island
Canadian Wildlife Service
P.O. Box 1590
Sackville, N.B.
E0A 3C0

Newfoundland
Canadian Wildlife Service
Room 611
Sir Humphrey Gilbert
Building
St. John's, Nfld.
A1C 1G4

United States
Cornell Laboratory of
Ornithology
Cornell University
Ithaca, NY 14853

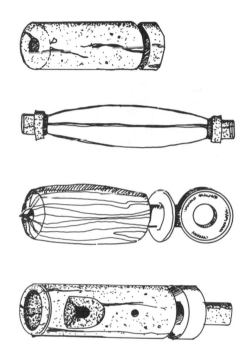

IMITATING BIRD CALLS

In spring, during breeding season when birds are most vocal, you can stimulate birds to call or approach you by imitating their calls. A number of birds have songs with the quality of a high-pitched human whistle. With practice, you can closely imitate these kinds of sounds.

Songbirds will also respond to commercial birdcalls. The Audubon Bird Call for Songbirds, made of pewter and wood, emits a twittering noise as it is turned. Although this is not the song of any particular species, songbirds do respond to the sound. Other calls available are the Hawk Screamer, the Owl Hooter, the Wood Duck Call, the Pheasant Call, the Crow Call, the Pintail Whistle, the Bobwhite, the Diver Duck, the Turkey Scratch Box, and the Gobble Box.

Songbirds will also respond to pre-recorded calls— either the ones you record yourself or those recorded on nature cassettes and records. You must take care not to call too often or too loudly, otherwise you may drive the bird away from its territory.

SPRING PLANTING

Spring is the time of year when you can plant food-bearing flowers and bushes. Scattered clumps of bushes with open spaces between them are more attractive to birds than solid vegetation. Birds require sunlight and prefer to be in an ecotone, the area where two levels of vegetation meet.

Flowers for Seeds
aster
bellflower
black-eyed Susan
cardium
chrysanthemum
forget-me-not
four-o'clock
larkspur
marigold
petunia
poppy
phlox
sunflower
sweet william
zinnia

Bushes and Trees for Fruit
bayberry
blackberry
blueberry
cherry
crabapple
cranberry
dogwood
eastern red cedar
firethorn
hawthorn
holly
honeysuckle
Japanese rose
mountain ash
plum
raspberry
Russian olive
tulip tree

SPRING PROJECTS

☐ Remove suet feeders in mid-March.

☐ Set out new nest boxes by April first.

☐ Remove feeding station at the end of April unless you are going to feed all year.

☐ Make a calendar of returning spring birds. Make it an annual event and refer to each year's calendar. You should find that the same types of birds return at approximately the same date. The order in which each type of bird returns each year should also be the same.

☐ Provide crushed eggshells for female birds. In spring, prior to egg-laying, eggshells supply a good source of calcium.

☐ Provide nesting materials. Cut wool, twine, and string into three-inch (8 cm) pieces and place outside on bushes and trees, in your suet dispenser, or near your nest box. Do not place these materials inside the nest box, or a bird might think the residence is already occupied and move on. Most birds prefer a clean, empty box.

☐ Grow your own sunflower seeds for next winter's feeding station. Choose the commercial variety of seeds rather than the garden-flower type. Plant in a sunny area near a fence or wall. You may serve the entire head once it has been cut off and sun-dried.

❏ Plant flowers to provide the birds with a natural source
   of seeds. See flowers listed under "Spring planting."
❏ Plant corn in a sunny area of the garden or in a flower
   pot. You may leave it standing and let the birds serve
   themselves or remove the husks to sun-dry the corn
   kernels.
❏ Plant a bush or tree to provide the birds with a natural
   source of fruit. See bushes and trees listed under "Spring
   planting."
❏ Join a bird-watching or naturalist club. Spring is when
   many clubs begin their new season. Most communities
   have a local organization and will often feature a junior
   club.
❏ Record bird sounds in the field.
❏ See what birds you can attract with commercial birdcalls
   or pre-recorded bird sounds.

IN SUMMER

In summer, birds thrive on the natural foods available,
such as insects, grains, and weed seeds. Sixteen hundred
species of birds eat nectar. That's 20 per cent of all birds. In
North America, sugar-and-water solutions will attract 53
species of birds. These include hummingbirds, orioles,
tanagers, grosbeaks, sapsuckers, and some warblers.

As temperatures climb, birds especially require water for bathing and drinking. To entice birds into your garden, make a bird bath with a shallow pan of water. (See directions under "Water" in the Fall section.) Cut up fresh fruit and serve on a tray. Fruit is nutritious and full of moisture.

Summer vacation may take you to a brand new location for bird watching. If not, it's a great time to join a local club for outings, or organize your friends for a hike or a visit to a nearby park or zoo.

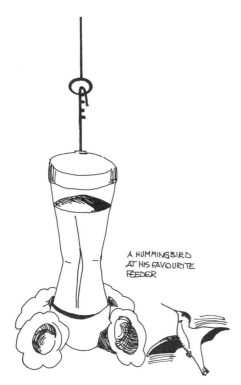

A HUMMINGBIRD AT HIS FAVOURITE FEEDER

SUMMER PROJECTS

☐ Cut up fresh fruit and serve on a feeding tray. Or, leaving the skin on, cut an orange into quarters. Thread the quarters on a string and hang them from the branches of a tree.

☐ Prepare a sugar-and-water solution for nectar-feeding birds. Mix one part white sugar and four parts water. (Never substitute honey which ferments easily and grows mold). With the help of an adult, boil the solution for one to two minutes. Cool before placing in the feeder. Store the unused portion in the refrigerator. Be sure to thoroughly clean the feeder and replace the solution every four or five days. Fungi and bacteria build up quickly in warm weather. If you have a problem with ants, coat the hanger part of the feeder with petroleum jelly or salad oil.

- ❐ Collect seeds from watermelons and cantaloupes for winter feeding. Rinse with water and dry. Then store in a dry place.
- ❐ Compile a list of the birds you saw on your summer vacation.
- ❐ Organize your friends for a bird-watching day in the neighborhood. The maximum number of people is twelve. If there are more, split up into two or more groups. Start as soon after sunrise as possible, while birds are most active.

YEAR-ROUND PROJECTS

- ❐ Assemble a scrapbook of newspaper and magazine articles on birds. Most newspapers feature a nature column. Be sure to enter the title of the article, the name of the paper, the date, and the page number for future reference.
- ❐ Assemble a picture file of birds. Collect pictures from newspapers, magazines, pamphlets, and advertisements. Organize the file in alphabetical order or file the picture according to country or locality. Enter the source and date of the picture for future reference.

❏ Assemble a photo album or a slide collection of birds, eggs, nests, and nestlings. Record the exact location where the photograph was taken, the date of the photo, and your name. Exchange copies of your photographs with your friends. *A Field Guide to Birds' Nests Found East of the Mississipi River*, and *A Field Guide to Western Birds' Nests*, both by Hal Harrison, will help you to identify your subjects.

❏ Collect stamps that feature birds. On December 6, 1967, the United States Postal Service issued its first bird stamp, with a picture of an egret. Since 1982, stamps featuring each state bird have been issued.

Canada's final airmail stamp, a Canada goose in flight, was the first Canadian stamp to feature a bird. It was issued on September 16, 1946. The northern gannet was featured in 1953; whooping cranes in 1955; the loon in 1957; Canada geese in 1963; gray jays in 1968; white-throated sparrows, the Ipswich sparrow and hermit thrush on two stamps in 1969; the peregrine falcon in 1978; the greater prairie chicken in 1980; and in 1986, the great blue heron, snow geese, the great horned owl, and the spruce grouse, each on its own stamp.

A list of bird stamps issued by the postal service in every country is recorded in these stamp catalogs:

Birds of the World in Philately, by Beverly S. Ridgely and
    Gustavs E. Eglajs.

Birds of the World on Stamps, by Willard F. Stanley, Beverly S. Ridgely, Gustavs E. Eglajs.

❏ Collect post cards that feature pictures of birds. Look for
    bird post cards in stores where post cards are sold. Other
    sources might be shops at conservation areas, state and
    provincial parks, zoos, and museums. Look for bird post
    cards whenever you travel, and get your friends and
    relatives to send them to you when they travel.

Chapter 3

ABOUT BIRDS

ARCHAEOPTERYX

ANCESTRY

The ancestors of today's birds are believed to have been animals that were swift runners whose first attempts at flight were probably flying leaps and parachuting jumps from tree to tree.

Archaeopteryx (meaning ancient wing) is the earliest-known bird from fossil records and dates from the Jurassic period (160 to 120 million years ago). It had many features of a reptile, but its feathers distinguished it as a bird. In addition to wings, it had a long, lizard-like tail edged with feathers, and its big toe turned back like that of modern birds, for gripping branches.

BIRD CLASSIFICATION

There are over one trillion birds in the world today. They are classified according to their common ancestry. The classification scheme used today—the Linnaean system—was developed by a Swedish botanist named Linnaeus in 1758. He gave every species two names, derived from Greek or Latin. The first name is the genus, the second is the species. Only the name of the genus is capitalized. For example, the American robin is *Turdus migratorius*.

SPECIES

Birds that resemble each other as closely as brothers and sisters are known as a species. The American robin is one species.

There are between 8500 and 9000 species of birds in the world. Birds continue to change and evolve, so experts often disagree when some members of a species have changed significantly enough to be considered a new species.

SUBSPECIES

Within the area where one species lives, there can be varieties or subspecies of that species. The American robin, for example, lives in the area from Alaska through Canada and the United States to southern Mexico. Because there are so many robins over such a large area, variations can occur within the species. For example, robins from eastern North America became known as the subspecies *Turdus migratorius migratorius*. Robins somewhat darker in color and living in northeastern Canada became known as the subspecies *Turdus migratorius nigrideus*. However, all are robins.

GENUS

Each species is a member of a larger group called a genus (the capitalized first name). All members of a genus are descended from a shared ancestral species. Members of the same genus have, for example, similar color patterns. The genus of the American robin is *Turdus*.

FAMILY

All genera (plural of genus) that share certain characteristics belong to one family. Ornithologists currently recognize 170 genera. Family members have many similar external features, like the same shape of bill, the same arrangement and length of wing feathers, the same pattern of scales on the legs and feet, and some similar internal structure. The scientific name of families ends in "-idae". For the American robin, a member of the thrush family, the name is *Turdidae*.

ORDERS

All families that are closely related belong to a single order. Altogether, there are 28 orders of birds. Families of each order have a common ancestor. Members of a single order have a similar internal body structure. For example, they have the same arrangement of bones in the head and the same shape of breastbone. There are also similar external characteristics, like the numbers of toes and tail feathers. The members of each order resemble one another more than they do the members of any other order. Names of orders end in "-iformes". The American robin belongs to the largest order, Passeriformes or perching birds. Passerines, as they are called, include more than 5000 species in 69 families.

In most bird books, the orders and families are arranged in chronological order to indicate the time of origin, from the oldest groups up to the most recently evolved. Passerines, which include all the families we think of as songbirds, are the most recently evolved order.

American robin
Species: *migratorius*
Genus: *Turdus*
Family: *Turdidae*
Order: *Passeriformes*

Orders, families, and species are the most useful categories for describing birds because they are clearer and less subject to change, owing to evolution, than genus or subspecies. In North America, there are 21 orders of birds, 75 families, and 950 species.

FEATHERS

What makes a bird a bird? Feathers! Only birds have feathers. Anything with feathers is a bird. No living creature can fly as long or as far as a bird. Flight enables birds to occupy a greater range of habitat than any other animal. Feathers make flight possible because they are light and elastic as well as resistant to wear-and-tear. Notice the great length of a flight feather in relation to how light it is. Try to break or tear a feather. Bend the tip to the bottom and watch it spring back. Feathers support themselves. This is an adaptation that eliminates the need for tail vertebrae, which would weigh down the bird.

STRUCTURE

Feathers have four parts: the calamus, the rhachis, the vane, and the hyporhachis.

The calamus, or quill, is a cylindrical hollow barrel with its base embedded in a follicle of skin.

The rhachis, or shaft, is filled with a white spongy substance called pith. The rhachis provides the feather with stiffness where support is needed, yet it is flexible closer to the tip, allowing the flying bird to change its direction in a split second.

The vane is made up of a two-sided web of barbs and barbules. The barbules have their own finer barbs called barbicels. A single feather may have several hundred thousand barbules and millions of barbicels. You can separate the web of barbs by running your finger down the feather against the grain, then bring them to-gether by running your finger back up. Birds re-hook the barbs and barbules when they preen their feathers.

The hyporhachis, or aftershaft, is located at the junction of the calamus and rhachis. This secon-dary feather is usually small and downy. However, in the emu and cassowary it is as large as the main feather.

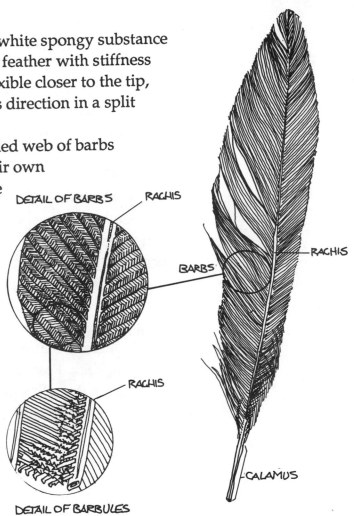

DETAIL OF BARBS

RACHIS

BARBS

RACHIS

RACHIS

CALAMUS

DETAIL OF BARBULES

TYPES OF FEATHERS

The outer feathers on a bird are contour feathers. They include the flight feathers of the wings and tail, and give a bird its shape.

Under the contour feathers are filoplumes, hairlike shafts with short tufts and barbs. Their purpose is not yet fully understood but they may help to control the movement of the contour feathers.

Many adult birds, especially those living in colder climates, have down feathers beneath their contour feathers to help insulate their bodies. Down feathers are soft and fluffy because they have a short shaft with barbs that do not interlock. This loose structure traps more warm air against the bird's body than contour feathers. Most young birds grow down before they grow contour feathers. The young of many game birds and waterfowl are born with down.

Down is more abundant in some species of birds than others. Waterfowl, for example, have more down than other birds because they require more insulation in water. Down provides better protection against cold than any material developed by humans. It is often used in sleeping bags, jackets and other clothing.

There are other more specialized feathers. Semiplume feathers are vaned like contour feathers but their barbules have no hooks like down feathers. They are found underneath contour feathers, usually along the sides of the abdomen. They provide warmth and bouyancy.

Powder down feathers are unique. They grow continuously and are never molted. The tips of these feathers break down into a fine powder. Powder down may help aid the removal of fish slime from some aquatic birds such as herons and bitterns. Birds that lack preen glands have more powder down to help waterproof and preserve the other feathers.

Bristles are like small, vaneless, contour feathers. They have only a few barbs at the base of an otherwise clean shaft. Many birds that catch

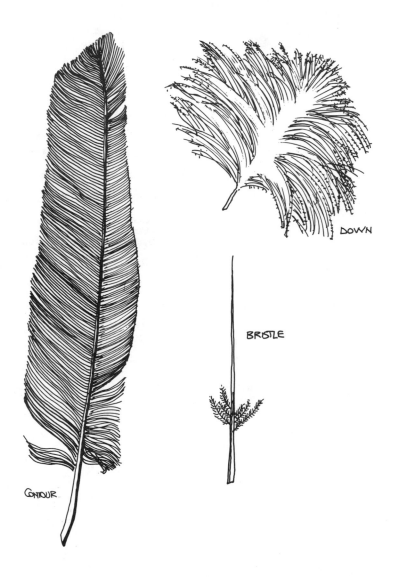

DOWN

BRISTLE

CONTOUR

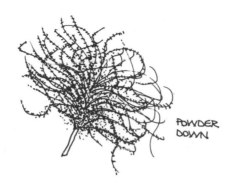

POWDER
DOWN

insects, including flycatchers and nighthawks, have bristles around their bills. Bristles sometimes occur around the eyes to form protective eyelashes, as in the ostrich, and around the nostrils to filter dust from the air.

FILOPLUME

SEMIPLUME

NUMBER OF FEATHERS

The number of feathers a bird has depends upon its species. Songbirds average between 3500 and 5000 feathers. A chicken has around 8000, a duck 12,000, and a swan approximately 25,000.

USES OF FEATHERS

Feathers have many uses. The primary one is to protect the body. Birds have thin, sensitive skin. They also have a higher body temperature than humans, between 104° and 112° F (40° and 44° C), and they need this protective layer for survival. Feathers keep birds warm in two ways: by their own thickness and by trapping air to add natural insulation. When birds are cold, they use the muscles connected to their feathers to fluff them up and entrap more air. When hot, birds compress their feathers to eliminate the air pockets.

A bird's plumage also protects the skin from water. Place a drop of water on a feather and watch the drop slide off. It runs off because the feathers are layered and waterproofed. The bird applies oil from the preen gland, which is located at the base of its tail. Some water birds, like the anhinga and the cormorant, lack waterproofing and spread their wings out to dry after swimming.

COLOR

Feathers come in a great variety of colors. Color is produced in two ways—by complex chemicals called pigments and by the structure of feathers that reflects light. The color of most feathers is the result of a combination of both pigment and structure. Pigments have other functions. For example, dark colors keep birds warm because they absorb heat from the sun. Dark pigments also give strength to feathers. Notice that the wing tips of many birds are reinforced with black feathers, an area where wear-and-tear is the greatest.

PROTECTION

One function of feather color is to give birds protection from predators. Many birds are camouflaged, and they blend in with their natural surroundings. Color is often a clue to their habitat. A quick look through a field guide will show many ducks, quail, grouse, shorebirds, owls, wrens, hawks, and sparrows that are shaded in browns to blend with their environment. Even more brightly colored birds, like the yellow and green warblers and vireos, are camouflaged among the leafy trees.

The females of many species are dull in color, so they will not attract attention while they sit on their nests. Young males of species in which only the male is brightly colored often do not get their bright feathers until their second summer, thereby improving their chances of survival. Young male grosbeaks, orioles, purple martins, and buntings resemble the female of the species in their first year.

COMMUNICATION

A second function of color is communication. Dull-colored birds are left alone by other birds. Bright colors seem to serve as a warning or a challenge. The vibrant red male cardinal defends his territory against other birds, whereas the brown female cardinal doesn't bother with other birds. When both the male and female of a species defend a territory, as blue jays and chickadees do, they are usually the same pattern and color.

Displaying plumage is part of courtship. Males use their body, wings, and tail feathers in displays to attract a female and to drive other males away from their territory.

CARE OF FEATHERS

Birds take good care of their feathers. Some bathe in water, others in fine dust. After a bath, birds attend to each feather individually. The bird reaches back to the preen gland, a small opening that secretes oil. The bird mixes the oil with its saliva and then draws its bill across each feather, cleaning and waterproofing at the same time. The preen gland provides more oil in aquatic birds, like ducks, whose feathers require more waterproofing. Oily feathers increase a bird's bouyancy in water.

MOLTING

Worn feathers cannot be repaired, so they are shed. This is called molting. Most birds molt once a year, after the mating season in late summer, just before autumn migration. Some birds molt twice in a year. The ptarmigan molts three times. Not all the feathers are lost at the same time. Generally, molting takes about six weeks. The feathers fall out and are replaced with new feathers in a regular sequence. There are exceptions: penguins molt in patches; geese and ducks lose all their flight feathers at once and are unable to fly for a short time. Some shorebirds, finches, warblers, and tanagers lose the brightly colored feathers of their breeding season and take on a somber winter plumage.

FLIGHT

Flight is the main characteristic of birds. It gives them safety and independence, enabling them to build nests and care for their young away from enemies; it allows birds to seek food, water, and breeding grounds over long distances, avoiding winter climates and enjoying two summer seasons.

Only a few birds cannot fly. These include the cassowary, rhea, emu, kiwi, ostrich and penguin. Chickens can fly, but not very well and not very far. Over millions of years the body structure of most birds has evolved into a superior structure for flying.

Flying requires a rigid air frame. Only the neck, tail, and wings are flexible. The ribs and backbone are joined together. This frame is both light in weight and remarkably strong. Birds have fewer bones than other animals. Bird bones are thin and most are hollow, strengthened by lightweight internal braces.

MECHANISM OF FLIGHT

If you look at a bird's wing in cross-section, you will see that it is similar in shape to the wing of an airplane. This shape is called an airfoil. The forward edge is round and blunt and tapers off to a narrow point in the back. The upper surface is convex—or curves out—and the lower surface is concave—or curves in. As a result, the upper and lower surfaces are unequal in length.

Air passing over the curved upper surface of the wing must travel farther than the air moving along the flatter

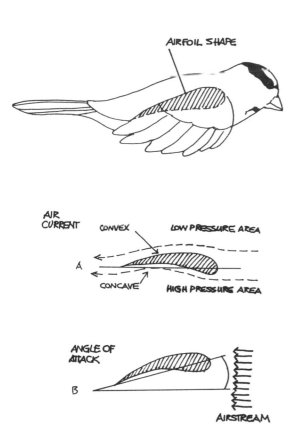

AIRFOIL SHAPE

AIR CURRENT CONVEX LOW PRESSURE AREA

A

CONCAVE HIGH PRESSURE AREA

ANGLE OF ATTACK

B

AIRSTREAM

surface beneath the wing. The air molecules above the wing move faster and spread farther apart. This creates a lower pressure above the wing than below. The greater pressure below the wing gives it lift. The flat or slightly concave underside of the wing increases the lifting power.

The amount of lift produced depends upon three factors: the shape of the wing; the speed the wing is moving through the air; and the angle of attack—the angle of the wing in relation to the airstream.

Birds have two ways of flying: they glide and they flap their wings. When gliding, the shape of the bird's wing provides lift because the bird is moving forward through the air. In flapping flight, the bird's wing acts as a propeller as well as a lifting surface.

GLIDING

A bird glides—without flapping its wings—when it falls from a higher to a lower altitude by taking advantage of the natural force of gravity. True flight is the ability to gain altitude. A gliding bird can increase its altitude by finding a pocket of air that is rising faster than the bird is falling. Updrafts are produced by wind deflected upward by objects such as hills, trees, and buildings. Birds also gain altitude by riding rising pockets of warm air called thermals.

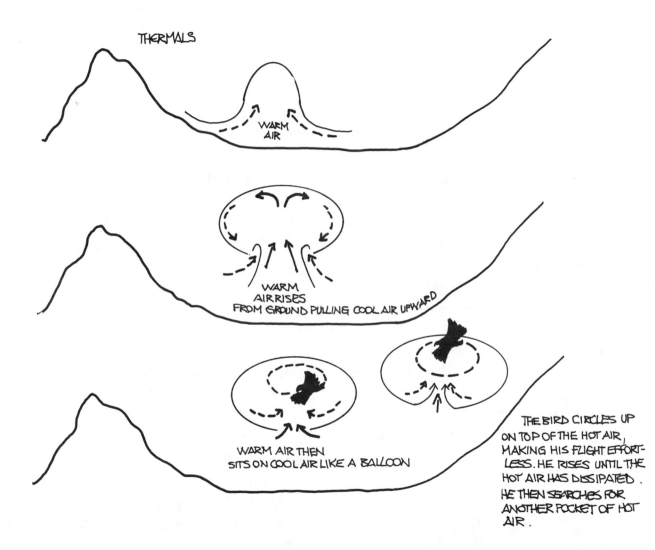

THERMALS

WARM
AIR

WARM
AIR RISES
FROM GROUND PULLING COOL AIR UPWARD

WARM AIR THEN
SITS ON COOL AIR LIKE A BALLOON

THE BIRD CIRCLES UP
ON TOP OF THE HOT AIR,
MAKING HIS FLIGHT EFFORT-
LESS. HE RISES UNTIL THE
HOT AIR HAS DISSIPATED.
HE THEN SEARCHES FOR
ANOTHER POCKET OF HOT
AIR.

Some species of birds, such as hawks, eagles, and vultures, are natural gliders. They are often referred to as "soaring" birds, being able to soar for structural reasons. They usually have broad wings and tails, which allow them to spend hours aloft without exhausting themselves. These birds are restricted as to where and when they can travel, because thermals are not produced over bodies of water or at night. The seabirds you see moving over water depend on wind. That is why they travel at lower altitudes, often just above wave-level.

FLAPPING FLIGHT

Birds use their muscles in powered or flapping flight. These powerful muscles represent about 15 to 30 per cent of the bird's weight. The largest pectoral or chest muscle contracts, pulling the wings forward on the downstroke from a raised position above the back. The wings are then pulled backward on the upbeat by a minor pectoral muscle that works like a pulley at the shoulder joint. The "arms" of the wings are used for lift, and the "hands"—or tips—of the wings are used for up, down, or forward direction. The forward downstroke pulls the bird along; the backward upstroke continues to lift the bird as the air slips freely through the flexible feathers of the parted wing tips.

Birds make adjustments when flying into the wind. If the angle of the wing is raised, the bird gains altitude but loses speed; if the angle is lowered, the bird loses lift but gains speed.

Flapping flight varies from species to species. The larger the bird, the slower the beat. A pelican flaps its wings 1.3 times each second; a red-tailed hawk 2 times; a pigeon 5 to 8 times; a mockingbird 14 times; a chickadee 24 times; and a hummingbird around 70 times.

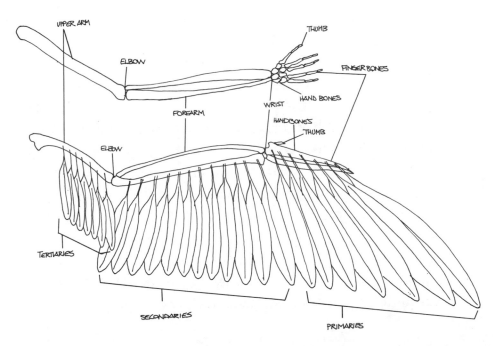

SPEED

How fast do birds fly? Swifts, the fastest of all flapping birds, have been measured in flight at 200 miles per hour (322 km/h). That exceeds the fastest running animal, the cheetah, whose top speed is 70 miles per hour (113 km/h). The more common average speeds of flapping flight are: songbirds, 20–37 miles per hour (32–60 km/h); crows 31–45 mph (50–72 km/h); plovers 40–51 mph (64–82 km/h); ducks 44–59 mph (71–95 km/h). The energy expended by birds in flight is six to twenty times greater than it is for other activities.

LANDING

When coming in for a landing, a bird drops its landing gear—its feet. It reduces its wingspread, causing it to lose altitude. The fall is slowed by a cupping action of the wings, which resists the air. The bird spreads and lowers its tail to land directly on target. For a split second, the wings are held high over the body and then neatly folded into place. You can observe this action of "wing lifting" in many shorebirds. Upon landing on a beach, they briefly hold their wings up over their backs before tucking them into place. Observe the precision of landing on-target shown by the birds arriving at your seed feeders.

HOVERING

Some birds are capable of hovering flight, the ability to stand still in the air. To do this, the bird spreads its tail to stall forward movement and moves its wings almost straight up and down. The sparrow hawk, which can be seen in open farming country, is nicknamed the windhover. This bird faces into the wind, beats its wings, and stays in one place while watching the ground for prey.

The hummingbird is specially equipped for hovering. The structure of its wings is different from that of all other birds except for its relative the swift. The hummingbird's wings are flexible only at the shoulder and can rotate nearly 180 degrees, like the wings of an insect. When hovering, the bird holds its body at an angle of 45 degrees. The wings sweep through a narrow figure-of-eight in a horizontal plane, resembling the action of helicopter blades. By changing the angle of its body, the hummingbird can fly both forward and backward and can rise straight up from the ground.

MIGRATION

In the Northern Hemisphere, bird migration can be observed throughout the year.

Approximately one quarter of the birds that inhabit

North America migrate twice a year. Most migratory activity occurs in the spring, between April and May, when the birds move to the north, to higher altitudes, or to the interior, and in the fall, from September to mid-November, when they return to the south, to lower altitudes, or to the seacoasts.

It is likely that birds have always migrated. Around 1000 B.C., Homer wrote about bird migration, and there are references to migration in the Bible. Aristotle (384–322 B.C.) recorded the migration dates of several kinds of birds.

Birds migrate in order to stay close to plentiful food supplies and ideal breeding grounds. Most species breed in summer when the weather is warm, days are long, and food is abundant.

HOW BIRDS MIGRATE

How birds know when and where to migrate remains a mystery. It has been suggested that environmental factors such as food supply, temperature, barometric pressure, the length of day, and the color changes of the leaves stimulate birds to migrate. But all these possible reasons, with the exception of day length, are too unstable to truly explain the regularity of migration.

Theories that birds find their direction from the sun, the

stars, the wind, and the earth's magnetic fields are inconclusive. Some people believe that birds find their way by means of landmarks and memory. However, young birds who have never migrated before fly south on their own and arrive at the same destination as their parents. Migratory habits may be inborn—that is genetically inherited. Chances are that this particular aspect of migration will remain a mystery forever.

REGULARITY OF MIGRATION

The most outstanding feature of migration is its punctuality within each species. Every year, the birds leave and return on almost the same date. Most birds migrate to the same location every year, some even to the same nest or nesting box. Unfavorable weather can delay small birds, but rarely larger ones.

ROUTES

The regularity of migration suggests that most birds adhere to an established air route or flyway. There are some exceptions: for example, it's known that waterfowl sometimes prefer a route 100 miles (150 km) or so east or west of the route they took the previous year. North America has four major flyways, which follow permanent geographical

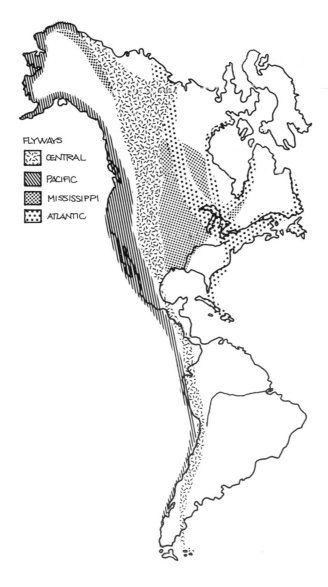

FLYWAYS
- [CENTRAL symbol] CENTRAL
- [PACIFIC symbol] PACIFIC
- [MISSISSIPPI symbol] MISSISSIPPI
- [ATLANTIC symbol] ATLANTIC

features: the Pacific Coast Flyway; the Central or Rocky Mountain Flyway; the Mississippi Valley Flyway; and the Atlantic Coast Flyway. These flyways are especially adhered to by waterfowl. Songbirds have more localized flyways. Migratory paths may be straight, curved, or irregular.

SPEED AND ALTITUDE

Observe that different birds travel at different heights and speeds. Those traveling the longest distances usually fly at greater speeds. Birds fly between 20 and 60 miles per hour (32 and 97 km/h); ducks and geese fly up to 50 miles per hour (80 km/h).

The majority of small night migrants fly between 2000 and 3000 feet (60 to 90 m). Shorebirds have been detected by radar at 20,000 feet (6000 m). Sea ducks, such as eiders and scoters migrate at just a few feet above water, but rise higher over land. Many land birds do just the opposite, migrating just a few feet above land and flying higher over water. Some birds, like jays and finches, fly in flocks above the trees, while soaring birds ride thermals several thousand feet or metres in the air.

Distance

For some birds, there is only a distance of a few hundred miles (about 500 km) between their summer and winter feeding grounds. Others travel thousands of miles or kilometres.The arctic tern travels for two months in a round trip that takes it from the Arctic to Antarctica and back again. The tern must average 75 miles (120 km) of flight each day to reach its destination on time.

Method of migration

Each species of bird has its own way of migrating. Robins and geese migrate in flocks, while others, such as hummingbirds, migrate alone. Small land birds, who are generally weaker fliers, avoid predators on their long flights to the tropics by migrating at night. Large birds such as hawks and herons, which use thermals to fly, can travel only by day. Daytime migrants also include the stronger fliers like swifts and swallows. They are able to outfly their predators and can catch insects while on the move. Other birds, including ducks, geese, and shorebirds, travel both at night and during the day.

HAWK MIGRATION

One aspect of spring and fall migration in North America is the migration of raptors—birds of prey that belong to the order Falconiformes. This order consists of eagles, falcons, harriers, hawks, osprey, and new- and old-world vultures.

Hawk migration is often concentrated along particular routes such as coastlines and mountain ridges. "Hawk watches" take place at a number of established points, including Hawk Cliff Raptor Banding Station at St. Thomas, Ontario and the Cape May Point State Park, Cape May Point, New Jersey. (See "Bird Observatories" in the next chapter.) The data collected by those studying hawk migration is used to assess the stability and health of raptor populations, which is believed to indicate the stability and health of all of nature.

The Hawk Migration Association of North America (HMANA) encourages amateurs to participate in compiling the migration data of raptors. Daily report forms and instruction pamphlets may be obtained by writing to them (see "Organizations for the birds" in the next chapter). HMANA publishes *A Beginner's Guide to Hawkwatching* and also makes available *Hawk Watch: a guide for beginners*.

All hawks use the rising pockets of warm air called thermals for flight. In the spring, when thermals are most abundant, hawks are more difficult for watchers to find because they fly over a wider range and at higher altitudes.

As early as the first week of February, turkey vultures head north; late in the month, buteos begin to migrate. The majority of spring migrations of raptors is in March, April, and the first two weeks of May.

The fall hawk watch begins in late August and early September. The most frequent sightings of raptors are from September 10 through October 31, although some continue to migrate into November and December. Generally, 8 A.M. to 11:30 A.M. and 2 P.M. to 5 P.M. are the best hours for hawk watching.

Tips for hawk watching:
• Face the direction the hawk is expected to fly (south in fall, north in spring).

- Before noon, watch along the horizon from one side to the other. Later in the day, look overhead and from side to side.
- Make observations from a distance; hawks can be identified up to several miles or kilometres away.
- Scan the edges of clouds. These are areas where thermals end.
- If there are no hawks, record the day's weather. This will tell you on what kind of day you are not likely to see hawks.
- When you spot a hawk, keep tracking it, as others will often join in. To assist you in identifying hawks, consult *A Field Guide to Hawks: North America*, by William S. Clark.

BIRD SOUNDS

All birds make sounds. (Storks and pelicans make no sounds outside of their breeding grounds, and six species of new world vultures only hiss.)

Birds are most vocal in spring, during their breeding season. Usually you will hear the males courting females and defending their territory from birds of the same species. The females of some species, like Baltimore orioles and rosebreasted grosbeaks, call less frequently. Many birds appear to sing for the sheer joy of it. Singing diminishes after summer nesting and ceases entirely during the late summer molt.

Birds vocalize for other reasons. Those that move in flocks, such as chickadees and Canada geese, call continuously to keep the flock together. Birds also vocalize to indicate aggression, anxiety, and alarm. These sounds are meant to warn their fellows of danger and to drive away enemies.

Some birds, including blue jays, brown thrashers, catbirds, crows, and starlings, imitate the calls of other birds. The reasons for this are not fully understood. One theory is that they hope to fool members of the same species into believing they are in another species' territory. The fooled bird then flies away, leaving the food supply to the imitator.

Birds make sounds in other ways beside singing: woodpeckers drum their beaks on trees; herons and owls snap their beaks together; kiwis stomp their feet; grouse create a drumming sound with their wings; and nighthawks, snipes, and woodcocks make noise by diving in flight.

COURTSHIP

Ordinarily, the males of each species migrate to the nesting grounds before the females arrive. The male selects the general territory in which the nest will be built, and the female usually selects the exact location. Spending most of his time in the territory he has selected, the male drives out other males of his species and migrating females of other species. Once the females of his own species arrive, court-ship begins. The male's objective is to convince one female to accept his territory. He does this by singing, defending the territory against other males, displaying his plumage, and behaving in a conspicuous manner.

The male usually sings in a place where the female can clearly see him. His song simultaneously indicates to the female a nesting area that will be guarded and warns other males to stay out of the territory.

The male will attack other males that enter his territory. If he is unsuccessful and is driven away by a stronger mem-ber of the same species, the female will accept the new suitor.

Many birds also display their plum-age as part of the courtship ritual. The male peacock

has brightly colored plumes, which he displays in full only during the breeding season. The nuthatch ruffles his tail and wing feathers as if to show them to the best advantage. The prairie chicken and sharp-tailed grouse can inflate a large air-sac at the throat beneath brilliantly colored skin.

Some birds use special body movements and antics to attract a mate. The horned lark and Wilson's snipe fly in peculiar circles in the air. The sharp-tailed grouse performs a stiff-legged dance. The cowbird compresses its feathers, then stands them on end, spreads its wings, hisses, and falls forward.

BIRD NESTS

A few birds make no nest at all. The penguin balances its egg on its feet and covers it with a fold of skin, even when it walks. The white tern lays its single egg on a tree branch. Some land birds and waterfowl lay eggs on bare ground and rock. Most birds however, do make nests to help keep their eggs warm and dry and safe from predators.

Most birds construct their nests with leaves, twigs, stems and moss. Some birds also use mud and saliva. A nest may be a simple structure or a complex one. How and where a nest is built can help identify the species that occupies it.

GROUND NEST MADE OF GRASS BRANCHES ETC.

GROUND NESTS

The simplest nests are depressions in the ground. These may occur naturally or be dug by the bird. Shorebirds and grouse make their own depressions and line them with pieces of shell, pebbles, and vegetation. Geese make more elaborate ground nests with a solid grass base.

ABOVE-GROUND NESTS

Nests above ground are safe from many predators, but the eggs can fall out. A great variety of nests are built in trees. They range in size and complexity from the tiny cup of the hummingbird, woven of moss, lichens, and spider silk, to the huge nest of the eagle, a massive pile of sticks that can be more than ten feet (3 m) tall after years of adding branches.

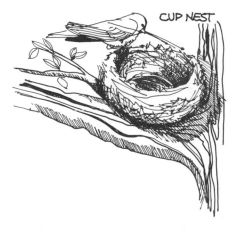

CUP NEST

CUP NESTS

One of the most common nests made both on the ground and above is the cup nest. A robin's nest is one example. The bird gathers a mass of material and works it into a bowl shape by scraping its feet backward and pressing with its breast. The edges of the nest are then built up by weaving in more material.

ROOFED NESTS

Some birds build up the sides of the nest and add a roof. Roofed nests offer greater protection from predators and weather. They are built most often by perching birds in the tropics, where the sun and rain are more severe and predators like snakes and mongooses are a threat.

HANGNESTS

African weaverbirds and Baltimore orioles make hangnests. These are tightly woven sacks of long grass and vegetable fibres. They are suspended from a tree branch by a long fibrous strand.

CAVITIES

Many birds, including chickadees, house wrens, and swallows, nest in natural cavities or those constructed by people (see "Nest boxes" in the previous chapter). Some build a nest within the cavity, while others lay their eggs directly on the floor.

To help you identify the nests you see, consult *A Field Guide to Birds' Nests Found East of the Mississippi River* and *A Field Guide to Western Birds' Nests*, both by Hal Harrison.

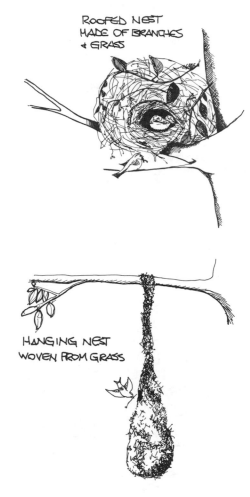

ROOFED NEST MADE OF BRANCHES & GRASS

HANGING NEST WOVEN FROM GRASS

EGGS

THE CLUTCH

The number of eggs laid by a bird at one time is called a clutch. The number of eggs laid in a clutch varies with each species. Some birds lay a fixed number of eggs. Other birds, like gulls, are able to lay extra ones if an egg is accidentally lost. The clutch size of birds of prey increases when food is plentiful and decreases when food is scarce. Generally, birds living in northerly latitudes, where summer days are longer, lay more eggs. Most perching birds lay from three to five eggs in a clutch and may nest two or three times in one season. Gulls, hummingbirds, and loons lay two eggs; auks, petrels and albatrosses lay one.

INCUBATION

Birds sit on their eggs to keep them warm until they hatch. This is called the incubation period.

Some birds share the duties of sitting on the eggs. Female pigeons incubate all night and the male all day. Waxbill parents incubate side by side on the nest. When only one parent incubates the eggs, it is usually the female. There are exceptions, though. The male emu and the male rhea incubate the eggs alone, and the female takes no part.

During incubation, the bird turns the eggs and rear-ranges them in the nest. Those on the outside are brought into the middle of the nest so that each egg will be warmed evenly.

The length of incubation varies with each species. Most small perching birds require from twelve to fifteen days; the domestic mallard incubates its eggs in twenty-eight days; the ostrich in forty-two days; and the emu between fifty-six and sixty-three days.

SHAPE, SIZE, AND COLOR

Birds' eggs are generally oval in shape. Owls' eggs are almost round, and those of swifts are oblong with rounded ends. Eggs vary in size according to the size of the bird. The smaller the bird, the smaller the egg. However, the eggs of shore birds are large in relation to the size of the bird.

The eggs of owls, woodpeckers, and kingfishers are usually laid in dark cavities and are white. The eggs of most other species are colored, spotted, or blotched. Perching birds usually have green or blue eggs. Eggs laid on or near the ground are often brown and spotted for camouflage.

PARASITES

Some birds lay their eggs in the nests of other species to avoid having to build a nest and raise their own young.

They are called parasites. Two well-known parasites are the cuckoo, found in Europe, and the cowbird, native to North America.

Parasites try to lay their eggs in the nests of birds whose eggs are the same size and color as their own. To fool the host bird, they will remove one of its eggs so that the clutch size remains the same. Frequently, the egg of the parasite hatches before those of the host bird do. The adopted nestling is able to outgrow the host bird's own young. It becomes stronger, taking more food, and often pushes the other chicks out of the nest.

YOUNG BIRDS

HATCHING

Between fifteen and forty hours before it hatches, a chick embryo forces a hole in its shell with the tip of its bill. This is called "pipping." At this time, the unhatched bird begins to breathe through its lungs.

When the chick is ready to hatch, it hammers a series of holes around the blunt end of the egg, starting at the first pipped hole, and moves counterclockwise in a circle. The young bird presses with its feet and heaves with its shoulders to force off the top of the shell and climb out.

For most species of birds, all the eggs in a clutch hatch

within several hours of each other, even though there could be hours or even days between the time that each one was laid. The eggs of birds of prey, owls, herons, cranes, swifts, and bee-eaters are deliberately laid at intervals and hatch at different times in case there is a shortage of food.

FEEDING

The offspring of birds that nest on the ground, including shorebirds, waterfowl, pheasants, and chickens, are ready to leave the nest soon after hatching. These chicks can usually feed themselves, although rails, grebes, and oyster-catchers are fed by the parents. Most are covered with down and their eyes are open. Their parents lead them to suitable feeding grounds and protect them from predators, and unfavorable weather.

Young songbirds, woodpeckers, pigeons, petrels, king-fishers, and hummingbirds are almost helpless when hatched. Their eyes are closed and there is little if any down on their bodies. They are weak and must be kept warm, or cool, depending upon the weather, for the first few days until their own bodies can regulate their temperatures.

Young birds feed in the daylight hours. It is a demanding task for both parents. For example, a pied flycatcher visits the nest with food thirty times each hour.

Adult perching birds and hummingbirds place food directly into the open mouths of their offspring. The young birds of penguins, pelicans, and cormorants retrieve food by thrusting their heads into their parent's mouths. If there is plenty of food, each chick is fed in turn. When food is scarce, some may go hungry and possibly die because the parents feed only a few to ensure the survival of at least some of the brood.

As soon as young birds can fly, they follow their parents and learn to search for food. Some will return to the nest at night, but eventually they will move farther away from the nesting territory in family parties or alone.

BANDING

Bird banding, or "ringing," as it is called in Europe, has been practised for centuries. Wild birds are captured and tagged with a numbered band placed on the leg. The bander records information about the bird, including when and where it was banded. As an effort to manage and conserve bird populations, banding is one of the most important ways of obtaining facts. Recovered bands reveal the numbers of birds, their annual production, lifespan, cause of death, behavior, movement, and distribution.

Banding also provides important information about bird

migration. It helps to map each species' travel route, to determine the distances between summer and winter feeding grounds, to measure the speed of migration, and to indicate the amount of time spent at breeding and wintering grounds.

Early banding was done with homing pigeons and with hawks used in falconry. The first modern record of banding dates from 1710. Rings were recovered on a gray heron in Germany. One ring had been placed on the bird in Turkey several years earlier. However, the bander remains unknown.

In North America, the first person to band birds was John James Audubon, the well-known naturalist and painter. In 1803, near Philadelphia, he tied silver-wire rings on the legs of a brood of phoebes. The following year, he identified two of the nestlings nearby.

Today, a systematic bird-banding program is being carried out in North America. The Canadian Bird Banding Office in Ottawa, established in 1923 and now administered by the Canadian Wildlife Service, works closely with the Bird Banding Laboratory in Washington, D.C., which is administered by the U.S. Fish and Wildlife Service.

WHO CAN BAND BIRDS

Only individuals authorized by these two agencies may band birds. Persons applying for a bird-banding permit must be 18 years of age. They must be recommended by two qualified ornithologists or persons actively holding banding permits. The applicant must be able to verify their ability to capture and handle birds without harming them, to identify them, and to keep accurate and detailed records.

HOW BANDING IS DONE

A permit allows trapping for the purpose of banding only. Trapped birds must be banded and quickly released. Ground traps in a variety of sizes and shapes are baited with food and water. For the many birds that cannot be enticed into ground traps, a specially trained bander can catch birds on the fly with a fine nylon net stretched between poles, called a mist net.

The bander continuously surveys the traps, carrying tools for banding and recording information. A trapped bird is taken in one hand and turned on its back. This relaxes the bird; many even go to sleep. Before the bird is banded, it is identified by species, age, and sex. To band the bird, its neck is held down gently with the little finger and the bird's left leg is held between the thumb and the forefinger. With the

free hand, the opened band is slipped onto the leg and
carefully closed with fingers or pliers.

TYPES OF BANDS

Both the Canadian and American banding agencies issue
identical bands to qualified banders. The bands range in
size from an inside diameter measurement of 2.0 mm (size
0) to 28.5 mm (size 9c). The band must be the proper fit—
small enough to stay on the bird's leg without hindering its
motion and large enough that it won't irritate the bird's leg.
The manual *North American Bird Banding,* (Canadian Wildlife Service, 1976), lists the correct size for each species.

The bands are made of aluminum, and each one is coded
with an individual number and a return address. Butt-end
bands are used for most birds and are applied to the lower
portion of the bird's leg by carefully closing the band with
pliers. Rivet bands and lock-on bands are applied to large
birds of prey since their strong beaks could easily remove
butt-end bands. A fourth type of band, a plastic leg band, is
color-coded and used in addition to other bands to allow
recognition of birds without having to recapture them.

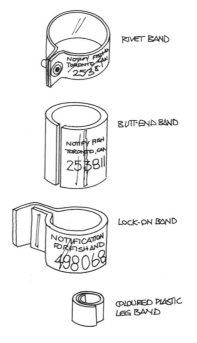

TERMINOLOGY

The following terms are used by bird banders:
nestlings—young birds banded in the nest

locals—young birds not yet able to fly very far

immatures—birds able to fly well but known to have
hatched in the year they were banded

subadults—birds hatched in the calendar year before the
year of banding

adults—birds hatched two or more years before the calendar year of banding

recovery—a banded bird shot and killed or found dead

foreign retrap—a trapped bird wearing a band from another station

repeat—a bird trapped within 90 days of being banded

return—a bird trapped after 90 days of being banded

Recovery of Bands

If you find a bird band or a dead bird wearing a band, remove the band, flatten it, and tape it securely to a piece of paper. Clearly print your name and address on the paper, the date the band was found, and the exact location where the bird was found. Include the species of bird, its age and sex (if possible), and how the bird was found, or how it died. Neatly print all the numbers and letters of the band on the paper.

If you find a live bird wearing a band, do not remove it. Record as much of the above information as you can and release the bird. Send the information to The Canadian Bird Banding Office, Canadian Wildlife Service, Ottawa, Ontario K1A 0H3, or to the Bird Banding Laboratory, Office of Migratory Bird Management, U.S. Fish and Wildlife Services, Patuxent Wildlife Research Center, U.S. Dept. of the Interior, Laurel, Maryland 20708.

If you send band information to the banding office, they will send you a certificate of appreciation telling when, where, and by whom the bird was banded. They will also send the bander a report on the bird.

ORGANIZATIONS

The interest in bird banding is so great in North America that four regional associations have formed to co-ordinate the efforts of individual banders, called banding co-operators. The Northeastern Bird Banding Association includes the New England states, Quebec, and the Maritime provinces; the Eastern Bird Banding Association covers the Atlantic coast states (except New England), New York, and Ontario; the Inland Bird Banding Association includes the territory between the Allegheny and Rocky Mountains, Manitoba, Saskatchewan, and Alberta; and the Western Bird Banding Association covers the Rocky Mountain and Pacific coast provinces and states. The work of these asso-

ciations is published regularly in news bulletins and
journals.

BIRD OBSERVATORIES

Bird banding on a large scale is one of the major activities carried on at bird observatories. A bird observatory is a research station. Its geographic location is carefully selected, always in an area where birds arrive regularly or at seasonal intervals in large numbers. The only buildings on the parcel of land house laboratories, a research library, and limited living quarters. (In the early developing years, some observatories have no buildings). There are few staff, if any. The work is done almost entirely by volunteer amateurs and researchers. In addition to bird banding and the recording and analysis of the bird-banding data, observatories research other aspects of bird behavior and individual species.

Bird observatories originated in Europe about a century ago. In North America, the Long Point Bird Observatory, established in 1960 by the Ontario Bird Banding Association, was the first of its kind. For the present, only a small number of observatories operate in North America. They are an excellent source of information and offer amateurs an opportunity to get involved and learn new skills.

Canada

Beaverhill Bird Observatory (BBO), P.O. Box 4943, Edmonton, Alberta T6E 5G8. Established in 1983 as the Beaverhill Lake Bird Banding Station. BBO is a natural breeding site for many water birds, and a stopover for migrating birds. The main activity is bird banding. Other projects include a daily count of birds on the lake, the keeping of nest records, shorebird surveys, breeding bird atlassing (recording where birds nest), putting up nest boxes, and studies of the behavior and habitat of individual species. Activities: field trips; training of volunteers; bird-banding workshops. Publications: newsletter; annual report.

Hawk Cliff Raptor Banding Station (HCRBS), c/o Don Fowler, 17 Fifth Avenue, St. Thomas, Ontario N5P 4C2. Established in 1969 by naturalist Marshall Field. HCRBS is a natural site for migrating raptors. On a record-setting day in September, 1961, it is estimated that 70,000 hawks were seen over Hawk Cliff. In the fall, between 10,000 and 20,000 raptors are observed daily. Over 40,000 have now been banded. The numbers of raptors are monitored in order to assess the status of each species, to determine whether they are becoming threatened or endangered.

Long Point Bird Observatory (LPBO), P.O. Box 160, Port Rowan, Ontario N0E 1M0 (519) 586-2909. Established in 1960 by the Ontario Bird Banding Association. The main program is the banding and monitoring of migratory birds. More than a quarter of a million birds, of about 240 species, have been banded so far. Many long-term and short-term studies of individual species are underway. Amateurs, province-wide, may participate in the Annual Ontario Bird Feeder Survey. LPBO administers the James L. Baillie Memorial Fund For Ornithological Research and Preservation, to encourage research by and/or involving amateurs. School-teachers and their students can enquire about going to the observatory for a variety of programs. Activities: workshops; outdoor classes; surveys; banding; Christmas bird count; annual birdathon fundraiser; lectures. Publications: newsletter (three times a year); annual report; *Directory of Co-operative Naturalists Projects in Ontario* (biannual); *Ontario Breeding Bird Atlas* (co-authored with the Federation of Ontario Naturalists); articles concerning their research are published in a number of scientific journals.

Prince Edward Point Observatory (PEPO), P.O. Box 831, Kingston, Ontario K7L 4X6. Established in 1975 by the Kingston Field Naturalists. Approximately 75,000 songbirds were banded between 1975 and 1981. Now the emphasis is on banding owls, primarily the saw-whets during autumn migration. Over 3000 have been banded since 1975. Occasionally, students are hired for summer projects.

Toronto Bird Observatory (TBO), Membership Secretary, 64 Coventry Crt., Richmond Hill, Ontario L4C 6A2. Established in 1978 by a local group of naturalists, the TBO is the first urban-based bird observatory in North America. The main program is the banding and censusing of birds migrating through the Toronto area. A trailer equipped as a laboratory is located on Mugg's Island, one of the Toronto islands, and winter banding is also carried on north of Newmarket. Activities: banding; censusing; study of the mortality of nocturnal migrants; wintering bird surveys; breeding bird surveys; instruction in bird banding, bird study, and census techniques. Publications: newsletter (four times a year); annual report.

United States

Cape May Bird Observatory (CMBO), P.O. Box 3, Cape May Point, New Jersey 08212 (609) 884-2736. Established in 1976 as the southernmost New Jersey Audubon Society Center. Known as one of North America's best year-round birding locations, this station has recorded more than 200 species on the Cape in a single day; more than 400 species have been seen on the peninsula. Best-known for flights of peregrines, merlins, ospreys, and sharp-shinned hawks, as well as warblers, owls, shorebirds, and waterfowl. More than 60,000 hawks and 1500 owls have been banded. Other projects include passerine research, migrating shorebird research, bald eagle survey, northern harrier and short-eared owl breeding surveys, nocturnal migration of owls survey, and surveys of nesting bird colonies. Activities: internships for teachers and college students; illustrated lectures; news releases; slide programs and manuals; hawk watches; field trips; workshops; bird walks; birding week-ends; general tips and information for birders; Cape May Birding Hotline (609) 884-2626, a 24-hour hotline detailing rare bird sightings from Cape May, updated weekly. Publications: *Peregrine Observer* (biannual newsletter); "Field Notes," a birding and natural history column in a local newspaper; *Hawk Watch: A Guide For Beginners.*

SURVIVAL
LIFE SPAN

The records of bird banders tell us that birds live short lives. Surviving the first year of life is the most difficult.

Approximately two thirds of all passerines (perching birds) die in the first year. Small birds live fewer years than large birds. Songbirds live an average of one to two years after their first year; wading birds and gulls live two to three years; large birds such as penguins live nine to ten years; and royal albatrosses live thirty to forty years. There are exceptions to these average life spans, but they are rare. The longest-known survival of a barn swallow is sixteen years; a crow, fourteen years; a cardinal, thirteen years; a black-capped chickadee, eleven years.

PROTECTION OF BIRDS

Since birds often cross borders and live in more than one country, they are protected by treaties between Canada, the United States, and Mexico. It is against the law to kill birds (except game birds in hunting season) or to trap them without a permit for the purpose of study.

Before there were laws to control the trapping and shooting of birds and the robbing of eggs from nests, people hunted birds for sport and profit. Hunters sold bird feathers for clothing, hats, and for stuffing pillows, and sometimes they killed birds for no apparent reason at all, without regard as to how many birds they killed, or how many were left.

Despite the laws that have been passed to protect birds, for some species it is too late. Their numbers have been greatly reduced. Birds of prey are one example. Birds are still the victims of natural predators and disease. Now other threats are shortening their individual life spans and diminishing their numbers.

One threat to the survival of birds is caused by the change, and in some cases the complete loss, of their habitat because of human infringement. Swamps have been drained and forests cleared to accommodate the expansion of roads and housing. Many birds are living at the extreme edge of their range or are being forced to change their range altogether. Insecticides have poisoned the food that birds eat. This can make birds sick and sometimes even kill them.

The survival of a number of species is now in jeopardy. There are five categories to describe species in danger as defined by the Committee on the Status of Endangered Wildlife in Canada:

Extinct: Any indigenous (meaning native to the area) species, formerly indigenous and no longer existing elsewhere.

Extirpated: Any indigenous species, no longer existing in the wild but existing elsewhere.

Endangered: Any indigenous species whose existence is

threatened with immediate extirpation or extinction throughout all or a significant portion of its range, owing to the actions of man.

Threatened: Any indigenous species that is likely to become endangered if the factors affecting its vulnerability are not reversed.

Rare: Any indigenous species that, because of its biological characteristics or because it occurs at the fringe of its range or for some other reasons exists in low numbers or in very restricted areas, and so is vulnerable, but is not yet a threatened species.

Chapter 4

BIRD TRIVIA

AGE
The OLDEST BIRD IN CAPTIVITY was "Kuzya", a male Andean condor. Kuzya arrived at the zoo in Moscow, U.S.S.R., in 1892 and died 72 years later in 1964. His age upon arrival at the zoo is unknown.

The bird with the LONGEST LIFE SPAN AMONG TAME BIRDS is the goose. The average age is 25 years.

BANDING
The FIRST modern RECORD of bird banding dates from 1710. A ring that was recovered from a grey heron in Germany had been placed on the bird in Turkey.

J.J. AUDUBON was the first person in North America to band birds. He banded a brood of phoebes near Philadelphia and identified two of these birds the following year.

The MOST NORTHERLY RECOVERY of a bird was in Novaya Zemlya, above European Russia, in May 1942. A tufted duck was recovered, which had been banded in London, England, in February of the same year.

The FIRST LONG-DISTANCE RECORD of an Antarctic bird was made in 1948. A giant petrel banded March 20, 1948, at Signey Island in the South Orkneys was taken alive on July 10, 1948, by a fisherman in Fremantle harbour in Western Australia. The bird had traveled more than 10,000 miles (16 000 km), averaging 150 miles (240 km) a day.

BIRD COUNT
American Stuart Keith has OBSERVED more than 5000 of the planet's 8700 species.

CALLS
All birds make calls with the exception of storks and pelicans which make NO SOUNDS outside of their breeding grounds, and six species of new-world vultures, which make only hissing noises.

The WORLD'S LARGEST COLLECTION of tape-recorded BIRD SOUNDS is housed at the Laboratory of Ornithology, Cornell University, Ithaca, New York.

EGGS

The LARGEST eggs belong to the ostrich: 6 to 8 inches (15–20 cm) long, 4 to 6 inches (10–15 cm) in diameter, 3.63 to 3.88 pounds (1.65 –1.78 kg) in weight.

The SMALLEST eggs are laid by the Vervian hummingbird: 0.39 inches (10 mm) long, 0.0132 ounces (0.37 g) in weight.

The SHORTEST INCUBATION period—the time between the laying of an egg and the hatching of the young bird—is 10 days. This is the incubation period of the spotted woodpecker and the black-billed cuckoo.

The LONGEST INCUBATION period is between 75 and 82 days. This is the incubation period of the wandering albatross.

FEATHERS

The LONGEST feathers belong to the male onagador, a bird bred in Southwestern Japan. One such tail feather measured in 1973 was 34 feet 9 1/2 inches (10.6 m) long.

FLIGHT

The LONGEST recorded flight was 14,000 miles (22 000 km), flown by an Arctic tern. It was banded on July 5, 1955, on the Arctic coast of Russia and captured May 15, 1956, near Fremantle, Australia.

The LONGEST TRANS-OCEANIC flight was 7000 miles (11 200 km), flown by a black-headed gull. It was banded in East Prussia and recovered in Mexico.

The MOST RECORDED OCEAN CROSSINGS for any species have been by the kittiwake, which is able to survive by drinking salt water.

The FASTEST bird in FLAPPING flight is the swift, which flies at speeds around 60 miles per hour (100 km/h) and has been clocked at 200 miles per hour (320 km/h).

The FASTEST bird in DIVING flight is the peregrine falcon, recorded at speeds of 220 miles per hour (322 km/h).

The HIGHEST ALTITUDE is flown by the bar-headed goose which flies at 30,000 feet (9 000 m) to pass over the highest Himalayan peaks.

The LARGEST FLYING bird is the Andean condor, with an 11-foot (3.3 m) wing span.

FLIGHTLESS birds include the cassowary, rhea, emu, kiwi, ostrich, and penguin. Chickens can fly, but not very well and not very far.

NESTS

The LARGEST bird's nest on record was built by a bald eagle near St. Petersburg, Florida. It measured 9 1/2 feet (2.9 m) wide by 2 feet (6 m) deep. It was estimated that the nest weighed more than 2 tons (1800 kg).

SANCTUARIES

The World Center for Birds of Prey in Idaho is the WORLD'S LARGEST center for birds of prey.

Hawk Mountain, Pennsylvania, is the WORLD'S FIRST sanctuary for birds of prey.

Little Duck Island, off the coast of Maine, a nesting spot for black guillemots and open-sea birds, was the FIRST AUDUBON SANCTUARY, set up in 1900.

U.S. President Teddy ROOSEVELT FOUNDED the National Wildlife Refuge system in 1903 to protect endangered species and migrating waterfowl.

SIZE

The SMALLEST bird is the bee hummingbird. Adult males are 2.2 inches (5.5 cm) long. The bill accounts for half its length. The bee hummingbird weighs approximately 0.056 ounces (1.6 g). A butterfly weighs three times as much.

The LARGEST and the TALLEST bird is the ostrich, averaging between 7 and 8 feet (2–2.5 m) tall and weighing approximately 330 pounds (150 kg).

The swan's NECK is larger than its body. The long S-shaped neck contains 25 bones.

A pelican can hold more food in its BILL than it can in its stomach.

Chapter 5

SOURCES

GETTING INVOLVED WITH BIRDS

MUSEUMS

Museums frequently house bird specimens, including single feathers, parts of wings, and whole birds for close-up examination. They sponsor lectures and educational programs.

PARKS, NATURE RESERVES, CONSERVATION AREAS

Parks, nature reserves, and conservation areas are excellent places to observe birds. They are also a good source of local information and educational programs.

BIRD CLUBS

Bird clubs publish newsletters, organize field trips, hold monthly meetings, present slide shows, and sponsor lectures by experts. If you do not think there is a local club near you, consult Jon Rickert's *Guide to North American Bird Clubs* .

GOVERNMENT AGENCIES

Provincial and state wildlife agencies provide information on local programs and local bird species. They give information over the phone from their reference files and often distribute free posters and pamphlets on birds of their area.

NEWSLETTERS AND ANNUAL REPORTS

Bird clubs, bird observatories, and bird banding organizations publish newsletters and annual reports. Most are free upon request, or come with membership as is the case with bird clubs.

MAGAZINES AND NEWSPAPERS

Magazines range from those intended for the beginning bird watcher to the professional publications of ornithologists. They can be general, covering a variety of topics, or can deal almost exclusively with a particular facet of bird life, such as bird banding. For a list of magazines, consult a periodical directory like Ulrich's or Ayer's at your local library, under the subject headings "birds," "bird watching," or "ornithology." If the magazine is not kept at your library, write to the magazine and ask for a sample issue to acquaint yourself with the slant of the publication. Most newspapers run nature columns that feature local birding information.

ORGANIZATIONS FOR THE BIRDS

THE BIRDER BADGING PROGRAM, Canadian Nature Federation, 47 Clarence St., Suite 410, Ottawa, ON, K1N 9K1.

The Canadian Wildlife Service has developed a program to test the abilities of amateur birders. Eight levels of skill have been established. The program is administered by the Canadian Nature Federation and its affiliates. Badges are awarded for passing each level.

THE BROOKS BIRD CLUB, 707 Warwood Ave., Wheeling, WV, 26003.

A non-profit organization founded in 1932 to promote the study and enjoyment of birds and other aspects of nature. The club has over 1000 members in 38 states and 11 foreign countries with its headquarters in Wheeling, West Virginia. The club takes population and breeding surveys. The *Redstart* is its official publication. It also publishes *The Mail Bag*, a quarterly newsletter, occasional check lists, and special publications.

CANADIAN WILDLIFE SERVICE, Migratory Birds Branch, 351 St. Joseph Blvd., Hull, PQ, K1A 0H3.

A division of Environment Canada, the service publishes both general and scientific and technical publications. Many publications are distributed free, including *Bird Banding in Canada, Bird Feeders, Nest Boxes for Birds*, and a number of pamphlets on individual species of birds.

DUCKS UNLIMITED (CANADA), 1190 Waverley St., Winnipeg, MB, R3T 2E2.

DUCKS UNLIMITED INC., National Headquarters, P.O. Box 66300, Chicago, IL, 60666.

A private, nonprofit conservation organization dedicated to the perpetuation and increase of North American waterfowl. Some of their activities include the preservation of habitats, the banding of waterfowl, and the collection of data.

HAWK MIGRATION ASSOCIATION OF NORTH AMERICA (HMANA), P.O. Box 3482, Rivermont Station, Lynchburg, VA, 24503.

A volunteer, non-profit organization whose goals include adding to the knowledge and understanding of raptor migration across North America, conserving birds of prey and their habitats, and educating people unfamiliar with raptors. The association consists of a network divided into regions in Canada, the United States, and Mexico. Individuals may obtain daily report forms and an instruction pamphlet to participate in the collection of data. Reports from each region are then computerized and available for researchers. HMANA publishes the *Proceedings* of the North American Hawk Migration Conference, *A Beginner's Guide to Hawkwatching*, and a semi-annual newsletter. They sell major publications on raptors and rent slides, slide shows, and films. Available free are the daily report forms and instruction pamphlets for monitoring migration, a bibliography of children's books on birds of prey, and introductions to regional hawkwatching locations.

THE NATIONAL WILDLIFE FEDERATION, 1412 16th St. N.W., Washington, DC, 20036.

A nongovernmental, nonprofit citizens' organization whose goals are conservation of natural resources and protection of environmental quality.

THE OSPREY'S NEST, Colesville, MD, (301) 989-9036.

The first computer bulletin-board service, operated by Norman and Frances Saunders just outside Washington, DC. By phoning their number with your modem, you can access a world of birding information, everything from local sightings to tips on purchasing binoculars. The service operates 24 hours a day and costs the same as a long-distance telephone call.

NORTH AMERICAN BLUEBIRD SOCIETY, INC., P.O. Box 6295, Silver Spring, MD, 20906-0295.

A non-profit organization formed to increase the populations of the three species of bluebirds found in North America. The society studies bluebird ecology and publishes the results. Membership includes the society's quarterly journal, *Sialia*, and plans for making a bluebird nesting box. The society also holds forums and gives lectures.

THE PEREGRINE FUND, INC., 5666 West Flying Hawk Lane, Boise, ID, 83709.

A non-profit organization created in 1970. It is dedicated to preventing the peregrine's extinction and re-establishing the bird throughout its natural range. Since 1974, over 2600 peregrines have been released from the Atlantic to the Pacific.

RARE CENTER FOR TROPICAL BIRD CONSERVATION, 19th and the Parkway, Philadelphia, PA, 19103.

This non-profit organization, founded in 1973, was originally formed to protect endangered species. In 1986, the focus changed to the preservation of tropical birds. The Rare Center affiliated itself with the Academy of Natural Sciences in Philadelphia, a leader in research of birds in Latin America and the Caribbean. It now supports research, habitat protection and conservation education having to do with tropical birds.

SOCIETY FOR THE PRESERVATION OF BIRDS OF PREY, P.O. Box 66070, Mar Vista Station, Los Angeles, CA, 90066.

Founded in July 1966, this society is a private foundation concerned with the well-being of hawks and owls in the wild. It publishes a leaflet series on a variety of raptor topics and publishes a birds of prey newsletter, *The Raptor Report*. Inquiries on raptors are answered by the society's library archives. A narration, guide, and slide lesson for grades 5–7 may be borrowed by elementary teachers.

THE SUNCOAST SEABIRD SANCTUARY, 18328 Gulf Boulevard, Indian Shores, FL, 33535.

The Suncoast Seabird Sanctuary is a non-profit organization dedicated to the rehabilitation of sick or injured wild birds for return to their natural environment. Founded in 1971, more than 10,000 birds have been treated and released. The sanctuary sponsors an adopt-a-bird program and distributes two pamphlets: "The Care and Feeding of Orphan Song and Garden Birds," and "Help for Hooked Birds." The sanctuary is open seven days a week from 9:00 AM until dark.

THE WHOOPING CRANE CONSERVATION ASSOCIATION, P.O. Box 995, Indian Head, SK, S0G 2K0.

THE WHOOPING CRANE CONSERVATION ASSOCIATION, 3000 Meadowlark Drive, Sierra Vista, AZ, 85635.

The Whooping Crane Conservation Association is a non-profit, volunteer organization established in 1961 to encourage the use of artificial assistance to increase whooping crane populations and to educate the public in protecting these birds. American and Canadian Wildlife Services cooperate in an experimental project, taking eggs from nests and hatching them in incubators to develop a captive breeding flock. The association publishes a quarterly newsletter and maintains a library of books about cranes at the Saskatchewan Museum of Natural History in Regina, Saskatchewan.

THE WORLD CENTER FOR BIRDS OF PREY, 5666 West Flying Hawk Lane, Boise, ID, 83709.

In 1984, construction of The World Center for Birds of Prey expanded the scope of The Peregrine Fund, Inc. to include national and international conservation of birds of prey and other wildlife. Over 3800 raptors of 21 species of eagles, hawks, falcons, and owls have been bred. The center has studied 35 species of birds of prey, and assisted programs in 34 countries on 5 endangered species programs.

WORLD WILDLIFE FUND CANADA, 60 St. Clair Ave. East, Suite 201, Toronto, ON, M4T 1N5.

A registered charity that funds projects to conserve endangered species. They are one of the sponsors of "Operation Lifeline," an education kit for students in grades 4 to 8 that teaches about endangered species and tells how the students can become involved directly with saving wildlife.

NATIONAL AUDUBON SOCIETY, 950 Third Ave., New York, NY, 10022.

Founded in 1905 to protect birds, the society expanded through the study of bird life, and is now one of the largest and most distinguished conservation organizations in America, with 550,000 members. Its headquarters are in New York; there is an office in Washington, DC; there are 10 regional offices, 500 community chapters, 80 sanctuaries, four adult camps, five environmental education centers, and five research stations. Members of the society receive a bimonthly journal, *Audubon*. Audubon chapters in North America hold monthly meetings and sponsor field trips, programs, and seminars about birds and the natural environment. Most chapters also participate in the Christmas Bird Count, sponsored by the National Audubon Society. Write to the society for the chapter nearest you.

FOR KIDS ONLY

At present, there are only a few birding activities and organizations designed just for kids in North America. You might contact the ones we've listed for ideas in starting similar programs in your community.

Send us details of clubs, camps, programs, and activities not listed, and we'll include them in the next edition of this book.

CLUBS

Junior Gnats, c/o 560 Chester St., London, ON, N6C 2J9. Sponsored by the McIlwraith Field Naturalists in London, Ontario, members range from age 7 to 14. Activities: meetings (twice each month); field trips; bus trips; camping. Publication: *Junior Gnat News* (4 per year).

Kingston Junior Naturalists, c/o The Kingston Field Naturalists; P.O. Box 831, Kingston, ON, K7L 4X6. Sponsored by the Kingston Field Naturalists, members range from 6 to 16 years. They study all aspects of natural history. Activities: meetings; field trips. Publication: junior newsletter (three per year).

Macoun Field Club, c/o The Ottawa Field Naturalists Club, Box 3264, Station C, Ottawa, ON, L1Y 4J5. Sponsored by the Ottawa Field Naturalist Club; for grades 4 to 13. They study all aspects of natural history. Activities: meetings; field trips. Publication: *Little Bear*.

The Saskatchewan Natural History Society, Box 1784, Saskatoon, SK, S7K 3S1. An organization of naturalists and conservationists which includes a junior membership. Publication: *The Blue Jay* has some special features for junior naturalists.

Toronto Junior Field Naturalist Club, c/o The Toronto Field Naturalists, 20 College St., Suite 4, Toronto, ON, M5G 1K2. Sponsored by the Toronto Field Naturalists. Activities: meetings; field trips. Publications: junior newsletter (nine per year); *Flight*, an annual magazine produced by the junior members.

CAMPS

The Victor Emanuel Nature Tours Inc., Box 33008, Austin, TX, 78764. Directors Victor Emanuel and David Wolf operate Camp Chiricahua in Arizona every summer. Birders camp for 12 days in the Chiricahua mountains and nearby desert areas. Activities: bird watching; owling by night; hiking; tour of the Arizona Desert Museum; visit to bird sanctuary and research center in New Mexico. Ages 13-19.

The Youth Ecology Camp, Registrar, Audubon Ecology Camps & Workshops, National Audubon Society, 613 Riversville Road, Greenwich, CT, 06831. Located in Maine at the Hog island camp. Activities: study puffins and other seabirds; dredge up marine creatures from the ocean floor and tidal pool; general nature studies; night hikes; stargazing; special guests. June 18 to 29. Ages 10-15.

The Young Naturalists' Camp, c/o The Federation of Ontario Naturalists, 335 Lesmill Rd., Don Mills, ON, M3P 2W8. Located in a different ecological area each year. Activities: general nature studies; introduction to bird watching; field trips; early morning bird walks; identification of bird calls; making a bird checklist; bird breeding evidence. One week (usually end of August). Ages 10 to 15.

PROGRAMS

"Take Off, Eh!", sponsored by the Royal Ontario Museum, 100 Queen's Park, Toronto, ON, M5S 2C6. Part of the Saturday Morning Club. Activities: bird watching; field trips; building bird feeders and houses; egg decorating; egg disection; kite-making to imitate wings; examination of the museum's bird collection. Ages 8 to 10.

PROJECTS

International Crane Foundation, E11376 Shady Lane Road, Baraboo, WI, 53913. Adopt a Crane: Your school or class can adopt a crane by raising money for the International Crane Foundation (ICF). $100.00 helps hatch a chick in an incubator; $250.00 helps a chick to survive and fly by providing food; $1000.00 pays for an adult crane for the entire year. ICF will send you a picture of your crane.

Reach Out to Children Around the World: Cranes live on five continents. By raising money for ICF, educational materials can be sent to school children around the world to teach them how to help cranes survive. Any class donating $50.00 or more to ICF will receive a year's membership to ICF.

BIBLIOGRAPHY

BIRD BANDING

Bird Banding in Canada. Ottawa: Canadian Wildlife Service, 1982. (pamphlet)

North American Bird Banding. Ottawa: Canadian Wildlife Service, 1976. (pamphlet)

BIRD STAMP CATALOGS

Birds of the World in Philately, by Beverly S. Ridgely and Gustavs E. Eglajs. Milwaukee, Wis.: American Topical Association, 1984.

Birds of the World on Stamps, by Willard F. Stanley, Beverly S. Ridgely, Gustavs E. Eglajs. Milwaukee, Wis.: American Topical Association, 1974.

EGGS, NESTS, NESTLINGS

A Field Guide to Birds' Nests Found East of the Mississippi River (Peterson Field Guide Series), by Hal Harrison. Boston: Houghton Mifflin, 1975.

A Field Guide to Western Birds' Nests (Peterson Field Guide Series), by Hal Harrison. Boston: Houghton Mifflin, 1979.

FIELD GUIDES

The Audubon Society Field Guide to North American Birds. Vol. I., by John Bull and John Farrand, Jr. New York, NY: Alfred A. Knopf, 1977.

The Audubon Society Field Guide to North American Birds. Vol. II, by Miklos D.F. Udvardy. New York, NY: Alfred A. Knopf, 1977.

Birds of North America, by Chandler S. Robbins, Bertel Bruun, and Herbert S. Zim. New York: Golden Press/ Western Publishing Co., 1983.

A Field Guide to the Birds: A Completely New Guide to All the Birds of Eastern and Central North America, 4th ed., by Roger Tory Peterson. Boston: Houghton Mifflin, 1980.

A Field Guide to the Birds East of the Rockies, by Roger Tory Peterson. Boston: Houghton Mifflin, 1984.

A Field Guide to Western Birds PA (Peterson Field Guide Series), by Roger Tory Peterson. Boston: Houghton Mifflin, 1972.

Field Guide to the Birds of North America, by Shirley L. Scott, ed. Washington, D.C.: National Geographic Society, 1983.

Simon & Schuster Guide to Birds of the World, by Gianfranco Bologna. John Bull, ed. New York: Simon & Schuster, 1981.

HAWKWATCHING

A Beginner's Guide to Hawkwatching. Lynchburg, Va.: Hawk Migration Association of North America, 1982.

Field Guide to Hawks: North America, by William S. Clark and Brian K. Whealer. Boston: Houghton Mifflin, 1987.

Hawk Watch: A Guide for Beginners, by Pete Dunne, Debbie Keller, and Rene Kochenberger. Cape May Point, N.J.: Cape May Bird Observatory, 1986.

NEST BOXES

102 Bird Houses, Feeders You Can Make, by Hi Sibley. Homewood, Ill.: Goodheart, 1980.

"Nest Boxes For Birds." Ottawa: Canadian Wildlife Service, 1977. (pamphlet)

30 Birds That Will Build in Bird Houses, by R.B. Layton. Jackson, Miss.: Nature Books Publications, 1977.

RECORDED BIRD SOUNDS

Field Guide to Bird Songs, 2nd ed., by Roger Tory Peterson. Boston: Houghton Mifflin, 1983.

A Field Guide to the Bird Songs of Eastern and Central North America. Cornell Laboratory of Ornithology, Cornell University. Boston: Houghton Mifflin, 1983.

A Field Guide to Western Bird Songs, Cornell Laboratory of Ornithology, Cornell University. Boston: Houghton Mifflin, 1961.

Nature Sounds of the Northwest, by K.J. Hall and Peter R.B. Ward. Vol. 1 Birds of the Dry Interior; Vol. 2, Birds of the Estuaries and Mountains.

Sound of Nature Series, by Dr. W.W.H. Gunn. *Songs of Spring; Warblers; Finches; Prairie Spring; Thrushes, Wrens and Mockingbirds*.

Voices of the Loon, by William Barklow.

Warblers of North America, Cornell Laboratory of Ornithology, Cornell University.

INDEX

S

Saskatchewan Natural History Society, The, 125
seeds: collecting, 40, 41, 58; sunflower, 36–37, 55
semiplume, 67–68
singing, 87–88
size, bird identification by, 27–28
Society for the Preservation of Birds of Prey, 122
songs, *see* recordings,
species, 62, 65
spring planting, 53–54
spring projects, 55–56
speed of flight, 79
speed of migration, 83–84
squirrel guard, 49
string foods, 44–45
subadults, 101
subspecies, 62–63
sugar solution, preparation of, 57–58
suet, 39, 47
suet container, 39, 55
summer projects, 57–58

Suncoast Seabird Sanctuary, The, 123
sunflower seeds, 36–37, 55
survival, 107–110

T

tape recorder, 17
telephoto lens, 16
thermals, 75–77, 86
Toronto Bird Observatory, 106
Toronto Junior Field Naturalist Club, 125
treaties, 108

U

updrafts, 75–77

V

vane, 65, 66
Victory Emanuel Nature Tours, The, 125–126
voice identification, 31–33

W

water, 39
Whooping Crane Conservation Association, The, 123
wing lifting, 79
wings, 24
winter projects, 44–46
World Center for Birds of Prey, The, 124
World Wildlife Fund Canada, 122

Y

young birds: feeding, 96–97; hatching, 95–96. *see also* nestlings
Youth Ecology Camp, The, 126
Young Naturalists' Camp, The, 126